PLAINWATER

ALSO BY ANNE CARSON

PLAINWATER

ESSAYS AND POETRY

ANNE CARSON

VINTAGE CONTEMPORARIES
Vintage Books
A Division of Random House, Inc.
New York

FIRST VINTAGE CONTEMPORARIES EDITION, MARCH 2000

Copyright © 1995 by Anne Carson

All rights reserved under International and Pan-American Copyright Conventions.
Published in the United States by Vintage Books, a division of Random House, Inc.,
New York, and simultaneously in Canada by Random House of Canada Limited,
Toronto. Originally published in hardcover in the United States by Alfred A. Knopf,
a division of Random House, Inc., New York, in 1995.

Owing to limitations of space, acknowledgments for permission to reprint previously
published material may be found on page 261.

Vintage is a registered trademark and Vintage Contemporaries and colophon are
trademarks of Random House, Inc.

The Library of Congress has cataloged the Knopf edition as follows:
Carson, Anne.
Plainwater : essays and poetry / by Anne Carson.—1st ed.
p.   cm.
ISBN 0-679-43178-0
I. Title.
PS3553.A766P58 1995
814'.54—dc20 94-42900
CIP

Vintage ISBN: 0-375-70842-1

www.vintagebooks.com

Printed in the United States of America

For Ben Sonnenberg / gentleman of the first water

CONTENTS

PART I

MIMNERMOS: THE BRAINSEX

PAINTINGS

fr. 1

What Is Life Without Aphrodite?

He seems an irrepressible hedonist as he asks his
leading question.

Up to your honeybasket hilts in her ore—or else
    Death? for yes
how gentle it is to go swimming inside her the secret
swimming
    Of men and women but (no) then
the night hide toughens over it (no) then bandages
    Crusted with old man smell (no) then
bowl gone black nor bud nor boys nor women nor sun no
    Spores (no) at (no) all when
God nor hardstrut nothingness close
    its fist on you.

fr. 2

All We as Leaves

He (following Homer) compares man's life with the leaves.

All we as leaves in the shock of it:
    spring—
one dull gold bounce and you're there.
    You see the sun?—I built that.
As a lad. The Fates lashing their tails in a corner.
    But (let me think) wasn't it a hotel in Chicago
where I had the first of those—*my body walking out of the room*
    bent on some deadly errand
and me up on the ceiling just sort of fading out—
    brainsex paintings I used to call them?
In the days when I (so to speak) painted.
    Remember
that oddly wonderful chocolate we got in East
    (as it was then) Berlin?

fr. 3

However Fair He May Once Have Been

In the offing he sees old age.

Yes lovely one it's today forever now what's that shadow
unzipping
    your every childfingered wherefrom?

fr. 4

To Tithonos (God's Gift)

For poor Tithonos.

They (on the one hand) made his chilly tears immortal
neglecting to tell him
    his eyes were not.

(853ff)

fr. 5

A Sudden Unspeakable Sweat Floweth Down My Skin

He gazes, perhaps he blames.

Sweat. It's just sweat. But I do like to look at them.
    Youth is a dream where I go every night
and wake with just this little jumping bunch of arteries
    in my hand.
Hard, darling, to be sent behind their borders.
    Carrying a stone in each eye.

fr. 6

Betwixt Thee and Me Let There Be Truth

Despite his professed cult of youth and pleasure,
he knows moral worry.

At the border crossing all I could hear was your pulse
    and the wind combing along my earbone
        like antimatter.

fr. 8

For Sun's Portion Is Toil All His Days

He looks to myth.

Look: up every bone every sky every day every you—
    He goes working His
way up blue earlobes from ocean goes
    thrown by rosesudden someone's
already tomorrow goes riding His bed of daysided gold goes
    skimming
sleep countries from west to east until sudden
    rosestopped someone's
already earliness opens the back of the clock: He
    steps in.

fr. 11

Would That Death Might Overtake Me

He sings of birthdays.

No disease no dreamflat famine fields just a knock on the
door
    at the age of threescore: done.

fr. 12

When Mountains Dove Sideways

He tells of Kolophon colonized from the mainland.

. . . When mountains dove sideways from Pylos
we came to Asia in ships
to Kolophon chiseled our way
sat down like hard knots
then from there
made a slit in the red river dusk and
took Smyrna
for God.

fr. 13(a)

So They from the King's Side

He sees the warriors move.

So they from the king's side when they got the order
went rushing—in their own hollow shields socketed.

fr. 14

None Such as Him

He looks to memory.

None such:
amid the butting bulls none such on the death flanks of
Hermos.
None.
Those elders who saw him saw the source points.
It stung God.
They say his spinal cord ran straight out of the sun.

fr. 15

He is troubled by words.

. . . in public words formed a clump in him.

fr. 16

Troubled.

. . . always the hard word box they wanted.

fr. 22

Half Moon

He awakens early.

Half moon through the pines at dawn
    sharp as a girl's ribcage.

fr. 23

Why does motion sadden him?

. . . a lame man knows the sex act best . . .

Mimnermos and the Motions of Hedonism

*I can swim like the others only I have a better memory than
the others, I have not forgotten my former inability to swim.
But since I have not forgotten it my ability to swim is of no
avail and I cannot swim after all.*

Kafka

Relocation among the substances that have us as humans is his
subject. People call it hedonism. That is like summing up
Kafka as a poor swimmer. If we consider the total somatosen-
sory system of Mimnermos's poetry, it is true we see the win-
dows glow in turn with boys and flesh and dawn and women
and the blue lips of ocean. It is true he likes to get the sun into
every poem. But the poet's task, Kafka says, is to lead the
isolated human being into the infinite life, the contingent into
the lawful. What streams out of Mimnermos's suns are the
laws that attach us to all luminous things. Of which the first is
time.

Although he scarcely uses the word, everything in his verse
bristles with it. Time goes whorling through landscapes and
human lives bent on its agenda, endlessly making an end of
things. You have seen this vibration of time in van Gogh,
moving inside color energy. It moves in circles (not lines) that
expand with a kind of biological inevitability, like Mimner-
mos's recurrent metaphor of the youth of humans as a flow-
ering plant or fruit. These plants grow as the light does, for

their life is one long day "knowing neither good nor evil" (fr. 10) until the sun slips over the rim and everything goes dark. He does not use the words for dark, but substitutes events: death, old age, poverty, blind eyes, empty rooms, vacated mind. It is as if the darkness *invents* these evils, which arrive for no reason except the light has gone. When you pass from sun to shadow in his poems, you can feel the difference run down the back of your skull like cold water. "And immediately then to die is better than life" (fr. 2).

Sun is the only pulse than runs by itself. While transiency grasps the rest of us through and through, Helios rides it as a cup across the sky (fr. 8). Mimnermos unblinkingly pretends to pity the god this endless motion. And that should tell us something about his hedonism.

For he only ever mentions two pleasures and he does not call them pleasures. There is no wine in Mimnermos's verse, no warm bath, no running animal, no cherries or silk or pale blue bones, no dice, no slapstick nights of song. It all takes place down behind the world somewhere in a state of static riposte, like a child talking himself through the night. Motion can stop, he is marveling. His hedonism seems to have struck a vein that was running through the times in which he lived— a kind of hunger for the motions of the self that we are mining still, though freshness is going out of the work. It is haunted from two directions at once, which we call pleasures to justify our hedonist calculus. Sex and light. Let us consider how they move him.

He "came to flower" (*floruit*, as the ancient biographers like to say) in the thirty-seventh Olympiad (632–629 B.C.). It is recorded that he originated in the city of Kolophon in Asia Minor, or else in the city of Smyrna somewhat northwest of Kolophon, or else on an island called Astypalaia in the south Aegean Sea (but *astypalaia* means "ancient town" and may simply be a phrase from some poem no longer extant). Kolophon had been colonized from the Greek mainland before the eighth century and was, after its capture of Smyrna, the largest state in Ionia. Mimnermos tells some of the history of these events in fr. 12, but the account is not an historian's. There is no telling who "we" are in this poem, nor how we should apprehend these centuries flying past like a news clip. But then that is his point.

Also in fr. 14, we view the events of several epochs through a fast, bright dust of allusion to wars and former generations. It may be a poem about Gyges of Lydia, who pressed down the valley of the Hermos River against Smyrna and Kolophon early in the seventh century. It may be a call to arms against Alyattes's attack on Smyrna in the last decade of the same century. Mimnermos says he heard of these events from his elders who were eyewitnesses. But who is this incomparable man who fought on the plain of Hermos? His father? Grandfather? Some other footprint in the family romance? Also perhaps a complete fiction. At any rate, Mimnermos is plainly not interested in explaining historical references. He lets this brilliant shape move through time like a needle stitching together the two moments that compose nostalgia. *Then* and *now*. The fact that we are no longer in the light (by the time we look for it) is his subject. Insofar as we speak of Mimnermos's hedonism, we can refer to the subject as knowledge.

Or we could say this is the difference that hedonism makes: To locate joy and love and pleasure in the lap of light "knowing neither evil nor good" puts knowledge in the dark. It is a brain chemistry of naked injury and chronic despair that Mimnermos assumes for this moment of knowing. When Mimnermos *sees the light,* he sees it gone—like Jason in fr. 7 gone down his adversary road to the place where the sun god, Helios, and all the lights of the world lie stored in contrafactuality against us. "Nor would have . . ." this fragment begins. Nor would the mechanical death of moments have come roaring down on us as darkness, had we not stopped to look round for the light.

Or do we stop because the light is vanished already? Mimnermos does not entertain philosophical questions except technically. Consider the moment when old age darkens down on men and women in fr. 1. The sex act of these gentle beings is radically intercepted by an unscheduled metrical event. Exactly at the middle of the poem, which consists of ten verses organized in five elegiac couplets, time cuts through the narrative of flesh: *"but (no) then."* It is a very unusual caesura, a notably nonlinear psychology. We are only midway through the central verse of our youth when we see ourselves begin to blacken. We had been taught to believe there were certain rules of motion and collision that construct elegiac verse (e.g., "the dactylic hexameter avoids word end at midverse") but these are defied. We had been seduced into thinking that we were immortal and suddenly the affair is over.

Consider Tithonos (fr. 4), whose good faith in the institutions of mortality and gift exchange won him an answer to a question he did not know he was asking (nor would have). The story is so well known that Mimnermos barely alludes to its content: seduced by the goddess of the dawn, the beautiful youth Tithonos received from her a promise of immortality, forgetting that human life is not as a rule coextensive with human youth. There was no reward but endless old age for Tithonos's love of the first light. Like the gentle men and women of fr. 1, wondering too late about the length of the shadows, Tithonos is someone stranded in a technicality. In his case it is syntax, not metrics, that shapes the human predicament. The poem begins by setting out the first half of an unusually common Greek construction: the particle *men* ("on the one hand") is generally coordinated with the particle *de* ("on the other hand") to create a balanced sentence or two-part remark. It is as if some other side of Tithonos's story were about to be set in motion and carry him on past petrification. Sadly this does not happen. Of course the fragment may be incomplete. But then so is Tithonos.

Consider incompleteness as a verb. Every verb has a tense, it must take place in time. Yet there are ways to elude these laws. The Greek verb system includes a tense called aorist (which means "unbounded" or "timeless") to capture that aspect of action in which, for example, a man at noon runs directly on top of his own shadow. So in fr. 13(a) Mimnermos uses an aorist participle to describe how men move in war. Like acrobats of the psychic misdemeanor we call history, warriors qua warriors live hovering above the moment when action will stop. They are the receptacle of a charge that shoots itself toward the night side, spoor of its own explanation.

Mimnermos is a poet intrigued by beginnings and endings, but not in the usual way—who reveres noon as a study in true black: "socketed."

There is no afternoon in Mimnermos. Consider as sound play the difference between youth and age in his typical diction: repeatedly applied to descriptions of old age is the adjective *argaleon,* which means "hard" and sounds like a fall of rocks down a dry ravine. Contrasted with it (e.g., in fr. 1) is the adjective *harpaleon,* which means "gentle" and sounds like a secret trout on the slip down the fathoms. It would be heartless to point out that, save for one consonant and the initial aspirate, these are the same word. When the soft *p* of *harpaleon* becomes the hard *g* of *argaleon,* all motions of day rigidify into the solid soul damage of nature's presupposition. Hedonism lies not beyond but *prior* to this—already forfeit.

Like sex, light is not a question until you are in the dark. Mimnermos has no answer to give. Instead (for he is a scholar after all) an epistemology: ". . . a lame man knows the sex act best" (fr. 23). This sentence, usually recorded among *dubia et spuria* in respectable editions, is thought to be a piece of proverbial wisdom learned from the Amazons one summer when he traveled in the Black Sea regions. Yes, there were still Amazons in those days, as there was a true physics of lust. "You are its ore," one of the big women said to him the day he left.

The Mimnermos Interviews (1)

M: It surprises me you came all this way

I: What a mud pond

M: You don't like rain

I: No let's get started can we start with your name

M: Named for my grandfather

I: The soldier

M: The great soldier

I: Can you tell us a little about him

M: He loved thunderstorms olives and the wilder aspects of life here he loved war

I: *None Such* is about him

M: I would have to say yes but you know a lot of it is invented fighting naked and things like that

I: I understand the text as we have it is merely the proemium to a much longer work

M: Well I don't know what you're reading over there nowadays those American distributors get some crazy ideas

I: I believe it's the standard edition (Diehl 2 volumes)

M: Don't get angry

I: I'm not angry I am conscientious

M: Like moss

I: What an odd thing to say have you ever been psychoanalyzed

M: Not so far as I know why do you ask

I: Moss is the name of my analyst

M: In New York

I: Yes

M: Is he smart

I: She yes very smart sees right through me

M: In my day we valued blindness rather more

I: Mystical

M: Mystical I don't think we had a word mystical we had gods we had words for gods "hidden in the scrutum [*sic*] of Zeus" we used to say for instance, proverbially

I: Doctor Moss would like that may I quote you

M: Ah the perfect listener yes I dreamed I would one day find her

The Interviews (2)

I: Within the last decade there have been many references from varied sources to the fact that the Western world stands on the verge of a spiritual rebirth that is a fundamental change of attitude toward the values of life after a long period of outward expansion beginning to look within ourselves once more can you comment on this

M: Secrets save me from dissolving

I: What do you mean

M: My separate existence down behind the world

I: Then you do believe in the unconscious

M: I see mankind reaching back by the millions to a time before my grandfather every morning when the sky gets blue they come streaming through my apartment

I: So as evidence of psychic life

M: Well no as the bottom we all start on the bottom start asking our way up

I: Dreams give us more than we ask

M: I'm not talking about dreams no one's dreams are of any use to anyone else

I: Why

M: They are merely experiments an experimental surface

I: But surely that involves at least let's say an organizing effort

M: Nothing takes place but the place

I: Are you serious

M: Just a telephone ringing in an empty house

I: Why not answer it

M: Why not keep moving it's true every epitaph calls out to the passerby but the marks are a trap the mourning is irrelevant I knew a man who dreamed his backside was made of glass and dared not sit down for 7 months

I: Freud says a dream is either a wish or a counterwish

M: Cagey

I: Or the disguises of these

M: Well eventually someone has to call a boat a boat you can't dismember everything

I: Dismember

M: Sorry I meant remember

I: Freud was named for his grandfather too

The Interviews (3)

I: [tape noise] . . . . something of your
    intellectual background *Where does he come from?* etc.
    perfectly reasonable

M: What are you digging for

I: Nanno

M: ———

I: Who is this person this chasm this lost event

M: ———

I: Considerable ambiguity surrounds Athenaios's assertion
    that in old age you became enamored of a flute girl by
    this name

M: ———

I: Kallimachos talks about Nanno or "the big woman" as if
    it were an epic poem on the founding of Kolophon no
    one understands this reference

M: ———

I: Strabo says you gave her name to a collection of love
    elegies

M: ———

I: Foucault speaks of the Unthought as a limit within which all actual knowledge is produced I'm groping here can we regard Nanno as some sort of epistemological strategy are we to look for a logic of Nanno

M: ———

I: Do you dream of her

M: No I dream of headlights soaking through the fog on a cold spring night

I: Now it is you who is angry

M: I'm not angry I am a liar only now I begin to understand what my dishonesty is what abhorrence is the closer I get there is no hope for a person of my sort I can't give you facts I can't distill my history into this or that home truth and go plunging ahead composing miniature versions of the cosmos to fill the slots in your question and answer period it's not that I don't pity you it's not that I don't understand your human face is smiling at me for some reason it's not that I don't know there is an act of interpretation demanded now by which we could all move to the limits of the logic inherent in this activity and peer over the edge but everytime I start in everytime I everytime you see I would have to tell the whole story all over again or else lie so I lie I just lie who are they who are the storytellers who can put an end to stories

I: You look so cold come closer to the fire

M: She used to get up first in the morning to light the fire it surprised me the young are seldom kind

I: Yet she was not a subject for you poetically I mean

M: I wrote her epitaph

I: I don't believe I know this piece

M: It was never published the family disapproved

I: I don't suppose you could

M: No

I: But

M: No

I: I wanted to know you

M: I wanted far more

PART II

SHORT TALKS

Introduction

Early one morning words were missing. Before that, words were not. Facts were, faces were. In a good story, Aristotle tells us, everything that happens is pushed by something else. Three old women were bending in the fields. What use is it to question us? they said. Well it shortly became clear that they knew everything there is to know about the snowy fields and the blue-green shoots and the plant called "audacity," which poets mistake for violets. I began to copy out everything that was said. The marks construct an instant of nature gradually, without the boredom of a story. I emphasize this. I will do anything to avoid boredom. It is the task of a lifetime. You can never know enough, never work enough, never use the infinitives and participles oddly enough, never impede the movement harshly enough, never leave the mind quickly enough.

On *Homo Sapiens*

With small cuts Cro-Magnon man recorded the moon's phases on the handles of his tools, thinking about her as he worked. Animals. Horizon. Face in a pan of water. In every story I tell comes a point where I can see no further. I hate that point. It is why they call storytellers blind—a taunt.

On Chromoluminism

Sunlight slows down Europeans. Look at all those spellbound people in Seurat. Look at monsieur, sitting deeply. Where does a European go when he is "lost in thought"? Seurat—the old dazzler—has painted that place. It lies on the other side of attention, a long lazy boat ride from here. It is a Sunday rather than a Saturday afternoon there. Seurat has made this clear by a special method. *Ma méthode,* he called it, rather testily, when we asked him. He caught us hurrying through the chill green shadows like adulterers. The river was opening and closing its stone lips. The river was pressing Seurat to its lips.

On Gertrude Stein About 9:30

How curious. I had no idea! Today has ended.

On Disappointments in Music

Prokofiev was ill and could not attend the performance of his First Piano Sonata played by somebody else. He listened to it on the telephone.

On Trout

In haiku there are various sorts of expressions about trout—"autumn trout" and "descending trout" and "rusty trout" are some I have heard. Descending trout and rusty trout are trout that have laid their eggs. Worn out, completely exhausted, they are going down to the sea. Of course there were occasionally trout that spent the winter in deep pools. These were called "remaining trout."

On Ovid

I see him there on a night like this but cool, the moon blowing through black streets. He sups and walks back to his room. The radio is on the floor. Its luminous green dial blares softly. He sits down at the table; people in exile write so many letters. Now Ovid is weeping. Each night about this time he puts on sadness like a garment and goes on writing. In his spare time he is teaching himself the local language (Getic) in order to compose in it an epic poem no one will ever read.

On Parmenides

We pride ourselves on being civilized people. Yet what if the names for things were utterly different? Italy, for example. I have a friend named Andreas, an Italian. He has lived in Argentina as well as in England, and also Costa Rica for some time. Everywhere he lives, he invites people over for supper. It is a lot of work. Artichoke pasta. Peaches. His deep smile never fades. What if the proper name for Italy turns out to be Brzoy—will Andreas continue to

travel the world like the wandering moon with
her borrowed light? I fear we failed to under-
stand what he was saying or his reasons. What
if every time he said *cities,* he meant *delusion,*
for example?

On Defloration

The actions of life are not so many. To go in, to
go, to go in secret, to cross the Bridge of Sighs.
And when you dishonored me, I saw that dis-
honor is an action. It happened in Venice; it
causes the vocal cords to swell. I went booming
through Venice, under and over the bridges,
but you were gone. Later that day I telephoned
your brother. What's wrong with your voice?
he said.

On Major and Minor

Major things are wind, evil, a good fighting
horse, prepositions, inexhaustible love, the way
people choose their king. Minor things include
dirt, the names of schools of philosophy, mood

and not having a mood, the correct time. There are more major things than minor things over-all, yet there are more minor things than I have written here, but it is disheartening to list them. When I think of you reading this, I do not want you to be taken captive, separated by a wire mesh lined with glass from your life itself, like some Elektra.

On the Rules of Perspective

A bad trick. Mistake. Dishonesty. These are the views of Braque. Why? Braque rejected perspective. Why? Someone who spends his life drawing profiles will end up believing that man has one eye, Braque felt. Braque wanted to take full possession of objects. He said as much in published interviews. Watching the small shiny planes of the landscape recede out of his grasp filled Braque with loss so he smashed them. *Nature morte,* said Braque.

On *Le Bonheur d'Etre Bien Aimée*

Day after day I think of you as soon as I wake up. Someone has put cries of birds on the air like jewels.

On Rectification

Kafka liked to have his watch an hour and a half fast. Felice kept setting it right. Nonetheless for five years they almost married. He made a list of arguments for and against marriage, including inability to bear the assault of his own life (for) and the sight of the nightshirts laid out on his parents' beds at 10:30 (against). Hemorrhage saved him. When advised not to speak by doctors in the sanatorium, he left glass sentences all over the floor. Felice, says one of them, had too much nakedness left in her.

On Sleep Stones

Camille Claudel lived the last thirty years of her life in an asylum, wondering why, writing letters to her brother the poet, who had signed the papers. Come visit me, she says. Remember, I am living here with madwomen; days are long. She did not smoke or stroll. She refused to sculpt. Although they gave her sleep stones— marble and granite and porphyry—she broke them, then collected the pieces and buried these outside the walls at night. Night was when her hands grew, huger and huger until in the photograph they are like two parts of someone else loaded onto her knees.

On Walking Backwards

My mother forbad us to walk backwards. That is how the dead walk, she would say. Where did she get this idea? Perhaps from a bad translation. The dead, after all, do not walk backwards but they do walk behind us. They have no lungs and cannot call out but would love for us to turn around. They are victims of love, many of them.

On the Mona Lisa

Every day he poured his question into her, as
you pour water from one vessel into another,
and it poured back. Don't tell me he was paint-
ing his mother, lust, et cetera. There is a mo-
ment when the water is not in one vessel nor in
the other—what a thirst it was, and he sup-
posed that when the canvas became completely
empty he would stop. But women are strong.
She knew vessels, she knew water, she knew
mortal thirst.

On Waterproofing

Franz Kafka was Jewish. He had a sister, Ottla,
Jewish. Ottla married a jurist, Josef David, not
Jewish. When the Nuremberg Laws were intro-
duced to Bohemia-Moravia in 1942, quiet Ottla
suggested to Josef David that they divorce. He
at first refused. She spoke about sleep shapes
and property and their two daughters and a
rational approach. She did not mention, be-
cause she did not yet know the word, Ausch-
witz, where she would die in October 1943.
After putting the apartment in order she packed

a rucksack and was given a good shoeshine by
Josef David. He applied a coat of grease. Now
they are waterproof, he said.

On the End

What is the difference between light and light-
ing? There is an etching called *The Three
Crosses* by Rembrandt. It is a picture of the
earth and the sky and Calvary. A moment rains
down on them; the plate grows darker. Darker.
Rembrandt wakens you just in time to see mat-
ter stumble out of its forms.

On Sylvia Plath

Did you see her mother on television? She said
plain, burned things. She said I thought it an
excellent poem but it hurt me. She did not say
jungle fear. She did not say jungle hatred wild
jungle weeping chop it back chop it. She said
self-government she said end of the road. She
did not say humming in the middle of the air
what you came for chop.

On Reading

Some fathers hate to read but love to take the family on trips. Some children hate trips but love to read. Funny how often these find themselves passengers in the same automobile. I glimpsed the stupendous clear-cut shoulders of the Rockies from between paragraphs of *Madame Bovary*. Cloud shadows roved languidly across her huge rock throat, traced her fir flanks. Since those days, I do not look at hair on female flesh without thinking, Deciduous?

On Rain

It was blacker than olives the night I left. As I ran past the palaces, oddly joyful, it began to rain. What a notion it is, after all—these small shapes! I would get lost counting them. Who first thought of it? How did he describe it to the others? Out on the sea it is raining too. It beats on no one.

On the Total Collection

From childhood he dreamed of being able to
keep with him all the objects in the world lined
up on his shelves and bookcases. He denied
lack, oblivion or even the likelihood of a missing
piece. Order streamed from Noah in blue tri-
angles and as the pure fury of his classifications
rose around him, engulfing his life, they came
to be called waves by others, who drowned, a
world of them.

On Charlotte

Miss Bronte & Miss Emily & Miss Anne used
to put away their sewing after prayers and walk
all three, one after the other, around the table in
the parlor till nearly eleven o'clock. Miss Emily
walked as long as she could, and when she died,
Miss Anne & Miss Bronte took it up—and now
my heart aches to hear Miss Bronte walking,
walking on alone.

On Sunday Dinner with Father

Are you going to put that chair back where it belongs or just leave it there looking like a uterus? (Our balcony is a breezy June balcony.) Are you going to let your face distorted by warring desires pour down on us all through the meal or tidy yourself so we can at least enjoy our dessert? (We weight down the corners of everything on the table with little solid-silver laws.) Are you going to nick your throat open on those woodpecker scalps as you do every Sunday night or just sit quietly while Laetitia plays her clarinet for us? (My father, who smokes a brand of cigar called Dimanche Eternel, uses them as ashtrays.)

On the Youth at Night

The youth at night would have himself driven around the scream. It lay in the middle of the city gazing back at him with its heat and rose-pools of flesh. Terrific lava shone on his soul. He would ride and stare.

On *The Anatomy Lesson of Dr. Deyman*

A winter so cold that, walking on the Breestraat
and you passed from sun to shadow, you could
feel the difference run down your skull like
water. It was the hunger winter of 1656 when
Black Jan took up with a whore named Elsje
Ottje and for a time they prospered. But one icy
January day Black Jan was observed robbing a
cloth merchant's house. He ran, fell, knifed a
man and was hanged on the twenty-seventh of
January. How he fared then is no doubt known
to you: the cold weather permitted Dr. Deyman
to turn the true eye of medicine on Black Jan
for three days. One wonders if Elsje ever saw
Rembrandt's painting, which shows her love
thief in violent frontal foreshortening, so that
his pure soles seem almost to touch the
chopped-open cerebrum. Cut and cut deep to
find the source of the problem, Dr. Deyman is
saying as he parts the brain to either side like
hair. Sadness comes groping out of it.

On Orchids

We live by tunneling for we are people buried alive. To me, the tunnels you make will seem strangely aimless, uprooted orchids. But the fragrance is undying. A Little Boy has run away from Amherst a few Days ago, writes Emily Dickinson in a letter of 1883, and when asked where he was going, he replied, Vermont or Asia.

On Penal Servitude

Je haïs ces brigands! said an aristocrat named M-ski one day in Omsk as he strode past Dostoevski with flashing eyes. Dostoevski went in and lay down, hands behind his head.

On Hölderlin's World Night Wound

King Oedipus may have had an eye too many, said Hölderlin and kept climbing. Above the tree line is as blank as the inside of a wrist. Rock stays. Names stay. Names fell on him, hissing.

On Hedonism

Beauty makes me hopeless. I don't care why anymore I just want to get away. When I look at the city of Paris I long to wrap my legs around it. When I watch you dancing there is a heartless immensity like a sailor in a dead-calm sea. Desires as round as peaches bloom in me all night, I no longer gather what falls.

On the King and His Courage

He arose laden with doubt as to how he should begin. He looked back at the bed where the grindstone lay. He looked out at the world, the most famous experimental prison of its time. Beyond the torture stakes he could see, nothing. Yet he could see.

On Shelter

You can write on a wall with a fish heart, it's
because of the phosphorus. They eat it. There
are shacks like that down along the river. I am
writing this to be as wrong as possible to you.
Replace the door when you leave, it says. Now
you tell me how wrong that is, how long it
glows. Tell me.

PART III

CANICULA DI ANNA

What Do We Have Here?

1

What we have here
is the story of a painter.
It occurs in Perugia
(ancient Perusia)
where lived the painter Pietro Vannucci
(c.1445–1523)
who was called Perugino,
a contemporary of Michelangelo
and teacher of Raphael.
What do you need to know?
There are a few things.
In the fifteenth century
the Dukes of Perugia,
besieged by the forces of the Pope,
withdrew within the rock on which their city was built
and established a second,
interior city.
It came to be called La Rocca
and it did not save them
but it is still there.
The air inside it is astonishingly cold.
In the story that we have here
some philosophers of the present day
meet in conclave

upon the ancient rock of Perugia.
They seem to have commissioned,
for purposes of public relations,
a painter to record them
in pigments of the fifteenth century.
Perhaps they do so for historical reasons
(Perusia has a painted past).
Perhaps, a small verbal joke:
parousia needs a painted face.
You will understand
more of that than I do.
The painter, at any rate,
is not a happy man.
A woman, as usual, is the problem.
She too has a face
and a past
worth painting.
Does that look like enough for a story?
Vediamo.

2

I think that I would like to call her Anna.
When I arrived it was raining. Everyone
seemed to be annoyed with me.
I could not find
Anna's name on the list, they
produced another list, no, they drew

together in a circle, gesturing,
hopeless. I went out quietly.

Outside still raining.
Two things happened
(in the painting, a superposition of colors)
at once, both impossible.
I heard someone call Anna's name. I saw the sea.
Now, we are landlocked here.
Perugia (ancient Perusia)
is situated 1444 feet above sea level
on a group of hills overlooking the Tiber:
1000 feet below.
Its outline
is irregular. Within the medieval walls
are considerable remains of the lofty
terrace walls of the Etruscan period.
Some old Etruscan calling, "Ah . . ." in the rain,
is it possible? Doubled
and fell over the parapet,
gone by now in the sea.

Wild dogs, mouths dripping with such bloody
syllables, ebb and run over the ocean
floor down there.

Attenti ai cani.

3

They do not know her here. That is,
I am free to invent her! sweet
dogs.

4

I slept, woke, slept in a fever of dogs.
Let us make no mistake about the freedom.
Eyes burn backwards through two channels of skull.
I may choose
to take a color away from Anna, for example.
All the little blues and maroons.
Yes. Her cool soles.
Thin stench of bone burning
within, but
yes,
a dog may choose
to howl or not to howl.
Lei ha una ferita.
Cara ferita.

One has a wound.
It may not be serious.

5

There are other women here,
lifting their necks in the sun.
I hunger for Anna.
Passing a cubicle I saw a painting of her
and removed it to my room,
feverishly.
It proved to be a still life
of apricots and aqua minerale.
The glass has a crack
but it reminds me
of the times of day
at which she got hungry.

6

Famous phenomenologists of *tutta l'Italia*
have foregathered here.
They take things back to the sophists
then climb the stone stairs
for a heavy lunch.
Their foreheads are not so tall
as the foreheads
of French phenomenologists
but they are much more good-natured.

Lunch is the central meal of the day here.

7

E il treno giusto per Perugia?

Perhaps Anna will come today.
A train arrives at half past three.
Once she telephoned
from somewhere in the north.
I had not seen her since winter.
(In the painting, not white for
the snow, just bluish marks.)
Her answers on the telephone are notable
for what phenomenologists call "thickness."
In a voice one may hear
a rocky coast. Steep.
Brutal in winter. Justice?
We may look to trains for a certain
"unconcealedness of what it is," but not justice.

From the mineral azurite,
found in mines throughout Italy,
may be obtained a cool, pale blue pigment
slightly less costly than ultramarine,
yet by no means common.

"No trains were going where you were," she answered.

8

Anna is hesitating somewhere.

Maybe she is dreaming her dream.
It always comes to her
just before morning.
She is in a room,
and she is trying to close the door.
Arms and legs are forcing their way in.
Violent as lobsters. She thinks
this dream is very general.
I never heard of it
from anyone else.

9

It is perhaps not widely known
that a certain so-called Perugino
spent the years 1483 to 1486
covering with frescoes
that part of the Sistine Chapel
now immortalized by Michelangelo's *Last Judgment*,
which efforts were ruthlessly effaced
to make space for
his successor's more colossal genius.

10

The fact that Anna is somewhere
having coffee or a dream
is an assault on me.
I hate these moments of poverty.
What does man eat? ask the phenomenologists.
Like the dogs, names,
down there,
starving.

11

A phenomenologist from Louvain-la-Neuve
is telling us what Heidegger thought during the winter term
    of 1935.
There was an interrogation of art.
There was a circle to be made.
Anna was nowhere in question. And yet
all was not perfect. He warns
of a mistranslation (read "essence"
for "nature"). He moves his feet
on the marble floor.
The phenomenologist
has blood red feet.
Bared and feverish feet.
An attack.
He confronts the circle in Heidegger
with the circle in Hegel.

On the blue-black marble
his flushed feet confront
the beautiful white feet of Christ.
What is at issue,
the phenomenologist from Louvain tells us,
is a surplus. The other
phenomenologists are growing restless.
"It is too easy to say
Ich bin ich. It is too easy
to let these hot feet presuppose
the cool feet of Christ."

It is too easy to take colors away from Anna.

They break for cigarettes.
Everything improves. A cigarette
permits a natural attitude.
There may be an overcoming of subjectivity.
There may be lunch.
Or an interrogation of lunch.
No brushstroke
can be just cool.
Or we would eat
many more paintings.

12

One step back from the language
spoken by the phenomenologist
in his proper sense

is the language spoken by the phenomenologist
at lunch.
The dogs, Anna, eat one another's throats
down there (afternoons) for the heat.
If he is a true philosopher
and not just some shrewd businessman,
the phenomenologist loses no time
in working this proposition
into fundamental and grounded connection
with his own argument. In the painting
he has lifted his arm
and is reaching across
a snowy tablecloth
rendered in daubs
of blue and black.

13

Group portrait: a special commission.
I paint the philosophers at table and
on the way to Being.
The bottle is difficult. I attempt
a color invented by Cimabue.
The phenomenologists engage in dialectic
about wine as vinegar.
To render the throat holes
(blackish red), I have acquired
sap of the tree *draco dracaena* (an expense

but the phenomenologists requested it)
or dragons' blood which, medieval legend
recounts, originally
soaked into the earth
during epic wars
of elephants and dragons,
thence to be gathered
by painters.

14

The phenomenologist from Paris hates mosquitoes
and carries a small electronic device
that lures the female mosquito to her death
by simulating the amorous cry of the male. Then,
to block the whining sound, he has pink earplugs.
As he sits in conversation
with the phenomenologist from Sussex
a mosquito is observed to enter.
The Englishman leaps to his feet,
calling, "Let us use the mosquito machine!"
and smashes the insect to the wall
with the device. It is the first sign
of wide ontological differences
that will open in the Anglo-French dialectic
here.

15

The phenomenologists are in each other's way today.
They cough, drop pencils.
"Your question, which is an excellent question . . ."
They smile.
"Crucial."
They point a finger.
"Very crucial."
Affection hovers.
"But you, you know that text very well. . . ."
Chairs scrape.
"My interpretation is fourfold. . . ."
"Twofold. . . ."
"On the way to . . ."
"I would like to say, *ja,* just the opposite. . . ."
"You could?"
A door slams.
"You can, but it's wrong."
Laughter.
"Our understanding of it must come from . . ."
"From art . . ."
"Ahistorically . . ."
"From the *Spiegel* interview . . ."
Papers fall.
"Could we ask you to translate?"
"I would say, the *Geschichte* of *Geschichte*. . . ."
A woman asks for matches.

"Not tragic . . ."
"A sort of phenomenological pastoral . . ."
"Heidegger, *ja,* liked farmers very much. . . ."

16

On the day Anna was married
her father traveled from a foreign country
to dissuade her.
Ran up the aisle with his hands full of money,
everyone turned.
After the ceremony the two of them
strode back down the aisle arguing,
and left the bridegroom at the altar,
unheard over the dogs.
In the official portraits
it remains unclear to me
who is who.

(For the coins
the painter appears to have used
verdigris, an acetate of copper
that produces a cool, rather
bluish tone
unless tempered with saffron
to bring it closer
to true green.)

17

It was the tender Pietro Vannucci,
alias Perugino,
who bid the mirrors be set up
inside La Rocca,
some phenomenologists allege.
(Others say
Vassilacchi, alias Alienese,
but this is unlikely to be true.)
He needed a place to work.
He needed a place to go
to get away from the talk on the streets—
Buonarroti, Buonarroti all day long.

18

I was practicing my Italian in the bar
(the mosquitoes prefer to bite the eyes of the foreigners)
when Anna came.
An event that threw me into bad temper.
I told her
to sleep with her eyes open
and left for a walk.
Ich bin ich.

19

One phenomenologist has a coughing fit.
Another begins to insist on the limitations of the text.
Tautologies, enigmata, drift in like an autumn.
The *Seinsfrage* is growing haggard.
Uncombed hair. Rough and cranky,
rubbing its eyes,
trying to make the Greek temple visible.
It bends forward; it takes tiny notes.
The color as color, the stone as stone.
Small syllables escape it.
"Sacredness is what is at issue."
Never mind that Greek temples
were butcher shops. What is at issue is,
there are two ways to visit Assisi.
One is naïve.
One loves Giotto. That is,
a being is inclined
to place itself
in front of another. (Except,
where we have to deal with crypto-Hegelians.
A crypto-Hegelian will try
to place himself *behind* Hegel.)
That is,
one is prior to two. (Of course,
the reverse is also true.)

One of the phenomenologists
appears to have brought his mother
to the seminar. (At least,
she is present in the painting.)
Hands in her lap, she regards
the speaker, infinitely
polite to us.

20

Powdered white lead for the long eyes of Perugino.

21

In Renaissance painting
every point in space is accounted for.
Here is a point,
Anna,
discoursing with the phenomenologist from Wiesbaden
and raising her eyes to heaven.
Standing
just outside their line of vision,
I slide my eye to the left.

Postmetaphysical myself,
I will be
unaccountable for the murder.

22

When you look at the painting you do not see the sound.
Barking all night, and
feet pounding
in the rock.
Barking like a long scald.
Barking.
Barking.
You see the faces.
The Dukes of Perugia,
full of sin.
You see each of them
slide an eye to the left.
To Anna.

Powdered white lead for the long eyes
of Perugino's
creatures.

23

The pure lines of Umbria
are a fever.
She knows that.
She knows I listen.
She pitches her voice
just lower than the
barking.

24

Working on her lecture in the library,
Anna observes a scorpion on the windowsill.
She withdraws to the breakfast room.
The phenomenologists inform her that she is mistaken.
"It is not a scorpion."
Besides that, she is fortunate.
"We are in Italy, not North Africa
where the bite of the scorpion
is fatal."
At length, the keeper of the Husserl archives in Berlin
agrees to accompany her upstairs.
He is struck. "*Ja,* you have a scorpion."
He pauses.
He turns to Anna. "You will leave the room, please?"
We cannot know what happened next.
The painter has used
colored earths to capture
the ugly stain on the windowsill.

25

Anna's dogs were running in the blood down there before
    we came.
Anna's dogs were angry in the fifteenth century:
The Dukes of Perugia built a city inside a rock.
Still they could hear the dogs.

Cannons were lined up on the wall
and aimed by use of mirrors.
Shots
missed the dogs and hit the Pope.
A chain of events proceeds in this way.
The artist
mixes a color. Without
the beautiful white throat of Anna
it would have been too dark
to paint
inside La Rocca.

26

I will tell you two things about Anna.
She loves to dance.
She was born with a defect of the heart called *hemolysis*
which causes blue clots of blood
to appear on her arms. The condition
is not painful.
It indicates that she was to have been
a twin.
Three things.
She killed her father.

27

In the sixteenth century there were lines and there were
    perspectives.

Vannucci in Perugia
hears Buonarroti bruited.
A hot summer, even in the hills.
In July, he lets his apprentices disperse
and sets out for Florence. Toward
the huge dark head and the fateful
conversation. It is a deeply shuttered
salon. Crowded. Vannucci, Buonarroti.
Buonarroti, Vannucci. Signor.
Exchanges of grudging praise.
A disagreement over perspective technique.
Loud. Louder.
B. ends by calling V. a "bungler in art"
(*goffo nell'arte*) and V. brings an action
for defamation of character.
The suit meets with no success
but his mortification spurs Perugino
to produce the chef d'oeuvre *Madonna e Santi*
for the Certosa of Pavia.
(The current story
that Raphael had a hand in the work
is unlikely to be true.)

Inside La Rocca
issues were simpler.
The barking has to stop.
Or there will be
men going mad.

Eyes slide to the left.

28

Along the sight line
of the beard
and the moving lips
of another man,
I watch her.
Let us make no mistake
about the freedom.
There are no lines visible in themselves.
There is no brushstroke
without color.
But the three-dimensional
knots of blue
on the arms of Anna
are an illusion produced by the painter.

29

The method of producing ultramarine
from lapis lazuli
was known in Europe only after the thirteenth century.
Before this it was imported, from across seas,
hence the name. Ultramarine
was available
in many grades of quality,
the finest of which is readily identified
by its cool cast and sparkle.

30

Some of Perugino's early works
were extensive frescoes
for the Ingesati fathers in their convent
(destroyed shortly thereafter in the siege of Florence).
The Ingesati
uneasily doled out to him
costly pigment of ultramarine.
Constantly washing his brushes
Perugino
acquired a surreptitious hoard of the color
which
he then restored to the prior
to shame his stinginess.

31

In the galleries above La Rocca,
concerts are held nowadays.
A pale green dead Christ
regards the cellist.
That is, he appears
to regard the cellist.
In fact, from under scant lashes
he studies his own arms
which float forward
with a power of their own.
Not uncanny, he seems to be saying,
but a thing to pay attention to,
for the moment.

The cellist is a tense
and obviously ailing man
attended by a deaf-mute dog.
It barks wildly from time to time (yellow)
making no sound.

32

Last night the dogs
killed a cock down there.
It crowed once (dark red) crazily,
far too early in the night.

. . .

They turned.
You could hear them turn.

As you can hear applause
turn in an audience
when the favored cellist
reappears for his bow.

As you could hear heads turn
when Perugino moved toward
Michelangelo
on a hot afternoon
in 1504.

Demented infant wandering in from the edge of the world.
One cry.
Grido.

33

Ordinarily,
the conversations of phenomenologists
are not worth overhearing. But
eavesdropping on Anna today
I learned—what next!—
she spent five years in a convent
during adolescence.

"I was callous."
That is, she knew
it broke her father's heart
but wanted time for philosophy.
The nuns were more callous.
They saw her moving
quietly back there
like a metaphysician in a novel,
glancing in.
Libertas ad peccandum et ad non peccandum.

Eyes left.

34

The first issue raised by the nuns
against Anna
was her arms.
She was suspected
of simulating the stigmata.

Second they wished her to give up philosophy.
That is, to give up
doing well at philosophy.

Third was her name.

35

"Do not hinge on me," Anna says.
"If you want my advice,
do not hinge at all."
One of our many discussions of freedom.
Anna goes dancing
with a phenomenologist
who is also a captain
in the military
(reserves).
When he sees some of his philosophy students
(to whom he refers as "the enlisted men")
dancing,
he retreats to the bar.
Anna dances joyously on alone.
I do not dance.
A dog has a choice.

"It spoils your eyes," Anna says,
"when you complain."
"I am not complaining."

The frescoes
have suffered grave deterioration
in the darkening of the light parts,
due to the chemical alteration of
white lead
because of
dampness.

36

Inside La Rocca they joked
that when the food ran out
they would hunt the dogs.
Then, that if
the dogs ran out they
would hunt each other.
Then they didn't joke.
Inside La Rocca
an ancient solution is debated.
An ancient category comes to light.

37

"The joy of living is to alter it."

Her wings gleam and fold shut.
She pauses
before an Etruscan boy
of green bronze. Leaves
nod heavily on his head.
He looks down, just
discovering
that his arms, if he lets them,
extend to the
soles of his feet.
His delight is total.

Graffiti covers the walls and tombs
of the Museo Archeologico.
I pass the time
photographing occurrences
of the name Anna, until
forbidden by an official.

Alter what?

38

In the convent
Anna took the name
Helena. The nuns
were content (Preserver
of the True Cross).
It was painful
for them to learn
she meant Helen of Troy.
And meant
the love of innocence.

39

Perugino, it is interesting to note,
was one of the earliest Italian painters
to practice oil painting, in which he
evinced a depth and smoothness

of tint, which elicited much remark.
In perspective
he applied
the novel rule
of two centers of vision.

40

To categorize
means to name in public:
κατηγορία
as many a phenomenologist
points out, at the outset of a seminar.
To categorize
is to clarify, often.
But not invariably.
Sacred filth, for example,
constitutes an ancient category
distressing to scholars
and other men of freedom
in the present day.
One continuous howl
by now. A being
made of raw sounds
joined at the stumps
and moving
as one form
down there.

Sound
that shines up as a laugh
and smells like blood
is another troublesome,
ancient
category.

41

Clouds of smoke in early morning
and men rushing about
with scaffolds and kindling
below the parapet.
I could have told them.
Dogs don't burn.
In July
of the year 1509
fires were lit outside La Rocca.
You could hear dogs
lurching through the flames down there.
Ocher
for heat and brutal suns and fever.
For flesh
gone transparent
where the fire passed through
he uses
black manganate over
filings of silver,

shavings of bone.
"Painting is a science," calls Perugino,
delirious,
through the smoke.

42

Silver leaf
must be cut with a knife on a leather cushion
and applied to the canvas
with a thin glue
of beaten and distilled egg white
called glair.
The technique
does not allow
for burnishing
afterward.

43

A curious system of exchanges
occurs within the painter's body
as he works. Touch
for touch, grace
for grace.
Murder thinks itself.
Pure lines of fever think themselves.

The painter chooses
where to stand
and the ritual
totters forward.

44

"No."
"Yes."
Inside La Rocca
an ancient dialectic
is under way.
"She is irrelevant."
"Essential."
"She is innocent."
"Innocence is a requirement."
"You exaggerate."
"You repeat yourself."
"She is not the sin."
"She appears in a painting of the sin."
"Deep in the background."
"Dead center."

45

Cristo morto.
It is a painting of a sacrifice.
The victim's arms

glow forward
strangely.
He regards them,
lowering
his eyes,
neither sleepy in death,
not delighted.

Perugino painted it in 1509,
mixing
with cypress resin
a sulfide of arsenic
known as orpiment
for the flesh tones.

Alter what?

46

The beloved's innocence
brutalizes the lover.
As the singing of a mad person
behind you on the train
enrages you,
its beautiful
animal-like teeth
shining amid black planes

of paint.
As Helen
enrages history.

Senza uscita.

47

Anna's father enlisted
for the beauty of the uniform
and served five years as a captain,
visiting Anna's mother nightly
by stealth over mountain roads.
When
a disorder of the blood
was diagnosed,
he chose to continue
to live as he liked.
"Drink hard, love deep, rest easy,"
he used to sing.
He grew thin: eccentric.
Thinner: monstrous.
Would not be seen by Anna.
At the birth of her son
she sent a letter, with
photographs, found
beside his body
the next day.

Important aunts
placed a long-distance call to Anna.
"You have killed your father."

48

On the last afternoon of the conference
the phenomenologists visit La Rocca.
They are surprised
that there is no entrance fee
for such a tourist attraction.
Then, by the cold inside.
Ruts of the rock breathe dark red air
from the fifteenth century at them,
making it hard to light cigarettes.
The phenomenologists cluster
in a passageway,
arguing
a point of *Dasein* from
the morning's seminar.
Some exit by a wrong door,
tumbling in sudden light.
A small phenomenologist
from Brussels
plans to write an article about the place
for a publisher in New York. He is eager
to ask the curator about the mirrors,
and about hoarding,

but the question
is not understood.
(She perceives him
to be inquiring
after the difficulty
of piloting herself about La Rocca
on high-heeled shoes, such as she
is wearing.
She assents vigorously. "*E difficile*.")

49

For very deep red,
use vermilion,
a sulfide of mercury.
Until the twelfth century
natural vermilion supplied most of Europe
with red pigment.
The discovery at that time
of a method for producing
vermilion in large quantities
by heating mercury and sulfur together
was an event of great importance
not only for artists
but for scientists as well.

50

Anna climbs stairs built on blood
to the aeroplane. Turns,
looks back, squinting (she
lost her sunglasses on our
trip to Assisi. Her husband
had bought them for her; and
had predicted she would lose
them.)
Misses me. Noon.
Pan on the tarmac casting no shadow.
Heat is pure motion.
I never saw her again.
The aeroplane
was exploded near Milan
by newsmen
simulating a terrorist incident.

Il mio sbaglio.
Il mio grido.

51

"No," said Perugino.
The darkness roared around him.
"Yes," said the Dukes of Perugia
and began to draw the huge stone of the door.

Ancient planets came south in a din
as they drove her
up the passageway
to the opening.
Anna did not hear
the dogs turn.

52

It was the last occurrence of such a ritual
in the city and archepiscopal see of
Perugia (ancient Perusia),
capital of
the province of Perugia,
which forms the entire *compartimento* of
Umbria,
and lies under the sign
of the Virgin and the Lion
(from which
cause it comes
that the city is called
Sanguinia
in some older accounts,
and its inhabitants
came forth strong in war,
they delighted in fish,
were humorous in speech,
neither luxurious,
nor indifferent to female charm).

53

Black for the pines,
black for the cypresses,
black for the thinking Christ.
But
silver rubbed
white for the bones
when we found her for
they stood
in the wounds like metaphysicians
quiet,
bloodless,
glancing
out.

Afterword

After a story is told there are some moments of silence. Then words begin again. Because you would always like to know a little more. Not exactly more story. Not necessarily, on the other hand, an exegesis. Just something to go on with. After all, stories end but you have to proceed with the rest of the day. You have to shift your weight, raise your eyes, notice the sound of traffic again, maybe go out for cigarettes. A coldness begins to spread through you at the thought; a wish forms. Perhaps it is something about me you would like to know— not that you have any specific questions, but still, that would be better than nothing. I could pour you a glass of wine and go on talking about the sun still upon the mountains outside the window or my theory of adjectives or some shameful thing I have done in the past, and none of us would have to leave just yet.

You do not know how this vague wish of yours fills me with fear. I have been aware of it from the beginning, I must be frank about this, I have worn it around my throat like a fox collar since the moment I said *"Vediamo."* Just then I felt your body tense for a story, and for something else. You tracked and peered and stalked it through page after page. Now here we are. Little snouts wake and bite in.

But could you tell me, what is so terrible about stepping off the end of a story? Let us look more closely at this moment that gathers at the place called the end. Up until this time, you have been fairly successful at holding back your tears, and suddenly you feel brokenhearted. It is not that you loved Anna, or look upon me as a friend, or hate your own life particularly. But there is a moment of uncovering, and of covering, which happens very fast and you seem to be losing track of something. It is almost as if you hear a key turn in the lock. Which side of the door are you on? You do not know. Which side am I on? It is up to me to tell you—at least, that is what other brave, wise and upright men have done in a similar position. For example, Sokrates:

> The man who had administered the poison laid his hands on him and after a while examined his feet and legs, then pinched his foot hard and asked if he felt it. Sokrates said "No." And after that, his thighs; and passing upward in this way he showed us that he was growing cold and rigid. And again he touched him and said that when it reached his heart he would be gone. The coldness by now was almost to the middle of his body and he uncovered himself—for he had covered his head—and said (what was his last utterance) "Krito, we owe a cock to Asklepios: pay it back and don't forget." "That," said Krito, "will be done, but now see if you have anything else you want to say." Sokrates made no further answer. Some time went by; he stirred. The man uncovered him and his eyes were fixed. When Krito saw this, he closed his mouth and eyes.

(Plato, *Phaedo* 118)

A cock for Asklepios: What a courtly gesture it is with which Sokrates ushers his guests out into the evening air, pointing the way for them (they have had quite a bit to drink). We hardly know such hospitality nowadays. And yet, having held you in my company so long, I find I do have something to give you. Not the mysterious, intimate and consoling data you would have wished, but something to go on with, and in all likelihood the best I can do. It is simply the fact, as you go down the stairs and walk in dark streets, as you see forms, as you marry or speak sharply or wait for a train, as you begin imagination, as you look at every mark, simply the fact of my eyes in your back.

PART IV

THE LIFE OF TOWNS

Introduction

Towns are the illusion that things hang together somehow, my pear, your winter.

I am a scholar of towns, let God commend that. To explain what I do is simple enough. A scholar is someone who takes a position. From which position, certain lines become visible. You will at first think I am painting the lines myself; it's not so. I merely know where to stand to see the lines that are there. And the mysterious thing, it is a very mysterious thing, is how these lines do paint themselves. Before there were any edges or angles or virtue—who was there to ask the questions? Well, let's not get carried away with exegesis. A scholar is someone who knows how to limit himself to the matter at hand.

Matter which has painted itself within lines constitutes a town. Viewed in this way the world is, as we say, an open book. But what about variant readings? For example, consider the town defined for us by Lao Tzu in the twenty-third chapter of the *Tao Te Ching*:

> *A man of the way conforms to the way; a man of*
> *virtue conforms to virtue; a man of loss conforms*
> *to loss. He who conforms to the way is gladly*
> *accepted by the way; he who conforms to virtue*
> *is gladly accepted by virtue; he who conforms to*
> *loss is gladly accepted by loss.*

This sounds like a town of some importance, where a person could reach beyond himself, or meet himself, as he chose.

But another scholar (Kao) takes a different position on the Town of Lao Tzu. "The word translated 'loss' throughout this section does not make much sense," admonishes Kao. "It is possible that it is a graphic error for 'heaven.'" Now, in order for you or me to quit living here and go there—either to the Town of Lao Tzu or to the Town of Kao—we have to get certain details clear, like Kao's tone. Is he impatient or deeply sad or merely droll? The position you take on this may pull you separate from me. Hence, towns. And then, scholars.

I am not being trivial. Your separateness could kill you unless I take it from you as a sickness. What if you get stranded in the town where pears and winter are variants for one another? Can you eat winter? No. Can you live six months inside a frozen pear? No. But there is a place, I know the place, where you will stand and see pear and winter side by side as walls stand by silence. Can you punctuate yourself as silence? You will see the edges cut away from you, back into a world of another kind—back into real emptiness, some would say. Well, we are objects in a wind that stopped, is my view. There are regular towns and irregular towns, there are wounded towns and sober towns and fiercely remembered towns, there are useless but passionate towns that battle on, there are towns where the snow slides from the roofs of the houses with such force that victims are killed, but there are no empty towns (just empty scholars) and there is no regret. Now move along.

Apostle Town

After your death.
It was windy every day.
Every day.
Opposed us like a wall.
We went.
Shouting sideways at one another.
Along the road it was useless.
The spaces between.
Us got hard they are.
Empty spaces and yet they.
Are solid and black.
And grievous as gaps.
Between the teeth.
Of an old woman you.
Knew years ago.
When she was.
Beautiful the nerves pouring around in her like palace fire.

Town of Spring Once Again

"Spring is always like what it used to be."
Said an old Chinese man.
Rain hissed down the windows.
Longings from a great distance.
Reached us.

Lear Town

Clamor the bells falling bells.
Precede silence of bells.
As madness precedes.
Winter as childhood.
Precedes father.
Into the kill-hole.

Town of Bathsheba's Crossing

Inside a room in Amsterdam.
Rembrandt painted a drop of life inside.
The drop he painted Rembrandt's stranger.
Dressed as a woman rippling.
With nakedness she has.
A letter in her hand she is.
Traveling.
Out of a thought toward us.
Her foam arrives.
Before her even when he.
Paints Rembrandt's stranger.
As Rembrandt he shows.
Him bewildered and tousled.
As if just in.
From journeys.
On tracks and side roads.

Sylvia Town

The burners and the starvers.
Came green April.
Burning and starving her.
Eyes pulled up like roots.
Lay on the desk.

Town of the Dragon Vein

If you wake up too early listen for it.
A sort of inverted whistling the sound of sound.
Being withdrawn after all where?
From mountains but.
They have to give it back.
At night just as.
Your nightly dreams.
Are taps open reversely.
In.
To.
Time.

Emily Town

Riches in a little room.
Is a phrase that haunts.
Her since the mineral of you.
Left.
Snow or a library.
Or a band of angels.
With a message is.
Not what.
It meant to.
Her.

Wolf Town

Let tigers.
Kill them let bears.
Kill them let tapeworms and roundworms and heartworms.
Kill them let them.
Kill each other let porcupine quills.
Kill them let salmon poisoning.
Kill them let them cut their tongues on a bone and bleed.
To death let them.
Freeze let eagles.
Snatch them when young let a windblown seed.
Bury itself in their inner ear destroying equilibrium let them
    have.
Very good ears let them yes.
Hear a cloud pass.
Overhead.

Entegegenwärtigung Town

I heard you coming after me.
Like a lion over the flagpoles and.
I felt the buildings.
Sway once all along the street and I.
Crouched low on my heels.
In the middle of the room.
Staring hard.
Then the stitches came open.
You went past.

September Town

One fear is that.
The sound of the cicadas.
Out in the blackness zone is going to crush my head.
Flat as a piece of paper some night then.
I'll be expected.
To go ahead with normal tasks.
Mending the screen.
Door hiding my.
Brother from the police.

Memory Town

In each one of you I paint.
I find.
A buried site of radioactive material.
You think 8 miles down is enough?
15 miles?
140 miles?

Luck Town

Digging a hole.
To bury his child alive.
So that he could buy food for his aged mother.
One day.
A man struck gold.

Death Town

This day whenever I pause.
Its noise.

Town of Finding Out About the Love of God

I had made a mistake.
Before this day.
Now my suitcase is ready.
Two hardboiled eggs.
For the journey are stored.
In the places where.
My eyes were.
Like a current.
Carrying a twig.
The sobbing made me.
Audible to you.

Pushkin Town

It has rules.
And love.
And the first rule is.
The love of chance.
Some words of yours are very probably ore there.
Or will be by the time our eyes are ember.

Town on the Way Through God's Woods

Tell me.
Have you ever seen.
Every tree a word once a.
Cloud over Bolivia.
Mountains were cowering once in an.
Old freight car the word for God's.
Woods.

Town of the Man in the Mind at Night

Twenty-five.
To four a.
Black.
Tinkle of the moon grazes.
It knocks.
It.
Off.
The blade.
Of night like a.
Paring.

Town of the Sound of a Twig Breaking

Their faces I thought were knives.
The way they pointed them at me.
And waited.
A hunter is someone who listens.
So hard to his prey it pulls the weapon.
Out of his hand and impales.
Itself.

Love Town

She ran in.
Wet corn.
Yellow braid.
Down her back.

Town of the Death of Sin

What is sin?
You asked.
The moon stung past us.
All at once I saw you.
Just drop sin and go.
Black as a wind over the forests.

A Town I Have Heard Of

"In the middle of nowhere."
Where.
Would that be?
Nice and quiet.
A rabbit.
Hopping across.
Nothing.
On the stove.

Desert Town

When the sage came back in.
From the desert.
He propped up the disciples again like sparrows.
On a clothesline.
Some had fallen into despair this puzzled him.
In the desert.
Where he baked his heart.
Were no shadows no up and down to remind him.
How they depended on him a boy died.
In his arms.
It is very expensive he thought.
To come back.
He began to conform.
To the cutting away ways.
Of this world a fire was roaring up.
Inside him his bones by now liquid and he saw.
Ahead of him.
Waiting nothing else.
Waiting itself.

Hölderlin Town

You are mad to mourn alone.
With the wells gone dry.
Starlight lying at the bottom.
Like a piece of sound.
Props hurtle past you.

Town of the Noon Stack

Midi.
Midi.
Midi.
Midi.
Midi.

Town of Greta Garbo

When my idol left it broke.
My back it broke my legs it.
Broke clouds in the sky broke.
Sounds I was.
Hearing still hear.

Town of Uneven Love
(But All Love Is Uneven)

If he had loved me he would have seen me.
At an upstairs window brow beating against the glass.

Town of the Exhumation

Old mother fingers coming down through the dark.
To rip me out my little dry soul my.
Little white grin that meets.
At the back.

Town A-Roving

There is no God but.
God out for God's.
Evening walk in the roaring.
Leaves the shudder forests.
The crops going dark the hearts.
Of gold as if they would break.

Thomas Town

Hand in hand into his mind never.
A thought came but that other.
Followed.

One-Man Town

It's Magritte weather today said Max.
Ernst knocking his head on a boulder.

Tolerance Town

Gold cup 1 woman 2.
Gold bowl 1 woman 1.
Gold bowl 1 woman 1.
Gold cup 1 woman 1.
Gold beaker 1 man 1.
Gold bowl 1 man 1.
Gold cup 1 woman 1.
Gold cup 1.

Judas Town

Not a late hour not unlit rows.
Not olive trees not locks not heart.
Not moon not dark wood.
Not morsel not I.

Bride Town

Hanging on the daylight black.
As an overcoat with no man in.
It one cold bright.
Noon the Demander was waiting for me.

Town of the Little Mouthful

Without arrows how?
Do I know if I hit.
The target he said smiling from ear.
To cut.
Through by the bowstring.

Freud Town

Devil say I am an unlocated.
Window of myself devil.
Say nobody sit.
There nobody light.
The lamp devil.
Say one glimpse of it.
From outside do the trick do.
The trick devil.
Say smell this devil say.
Raw bones devil say the mind.
Is an alien guest I say.
Devil outlived devil in.

Town of My Farewell to You

Look what a thousand blue thousand white.
Thousand blue thousand white thousand.
Blue thousand white thousand blue thousand.
White thousand blue wind today and two arms.
Blowing down the road.

PART V

THE ANTHROPOLOGY

OF WATER

Diving:
Introduction to the Anthropology of Water

I am a mendacious creature.

Kafka

Water is something you cannot hold. Like men. I have tried.
Father, brother, lover, true friends, hungry ghosts and God,
one by one all took themselves out of my hands. Maybe this is
the way it should be—what anthropologists call "normal dan-
ger" in the encounter with alien cultures. It was an anthropolo-
gist who first taught me about danger. He emphasized the
importance of using *encounter* rather than (say) *discovery* when
talking about such things. "Think of it as the difference," he
said, "between believing what you want to believe and be-
lieving what can be proved." I thought about that. "I don't
want to believe anything," I said. (But I was lying.) "And I
have nothing to prove." (Lying again.) "I just like to travel
into the world and stop, noticing what is under the sky." (This,
in fact, is true.) Cruelly at this point, he mentioned a culture
he had studied where true and false virgins are identified by
ordeal of water. For an intact virgin can develop the skill of
diving into deep water but a woman who has known love will
drown. "I am not interested in true and false," I said (one last
lie) and we fell silent.

Anthropology is a science of mutual surprise. I wanted to
ask him several questions, like whether he could tell me the

difference between heaven and hell, but I did not. Instead I found myself telling him about the daughters of Danaos. Danaos was a hero of ancient Greek myth who had fifty daughters. They loved their father so much it was as if they were parts of his body. When Danaos stirred in his sleep they would awaken, each in her narrow bed, staring into the dark. Then came time to marry. Danaos found fifty bridegrooms. He set the day. He carried out the wedding ceremony. And at midnight on the wedding night, fifty bedroom doors clicked shut. Then a terrible encounter took place. Each of forty-nine of the daughters of Danaos drew a sword from alongside her thigh and stabbed her bridegroom to death.

This archetypal crime of women was rewarded by the gods with a paradigmatic punishment. Danaos's forty-nine killing daughters were sent to hell and condemned to spend eternity gathering water in a sieve.

But yes, there was one daughter who did not draw her sword. What happened to her remains to be discovered. Clothe yourself, the water is deep.

Thirst:
Introduction to Kinds of Water

> *All things are water.*
>
> *(a sentence spoken by the ancient philosopher Thales*
> *one night when he had fallen down a well)*

I think it was Kafka who had the idea of swimming across Europe and planned to do so with his friend Max, river by river. Unfortunately his health wasn't up to it. So instead he started to write a parable about a man who had never learned to swim. One cool autumn evening the man returns to his hometown to find himself being acclaimed for an Olympic backstroke victory. In the middle of the main street a podium had been set up. Warily he begins to mount the steps. The last rays of sunset are striking directly into his eyes, blinding him. The parable breaks off as the town officials step forward holding up garlands, which touch the swimmer's head.

I like the people in Kafka's parables. They do not know how to ask the simplest question. Whereas to you and me it may look (as my father used to say) as obvious as a door in water.

Before leaving for Spain I went to visit my father. He lives in a hospital because he has lost the use of some of the parts of his body and of his mind. Most of the day he sits in a chair, hands gripping the arms. With his chest he makes little lunges against the straps, forward and back. His huge red eyes move all the time, pouring onto things. I sit in a chair drawn up beside him, making little lunges with my chest, forward and back. From his lips comes a stream of syllables. He was all his life a silent man. But dementia has released some spring inside him, he babbles constantly in a language neurologists call "word salad." I watch his face. I say, "Yes, Father" in the gaps. How true, as if it were a conversation. I hate hearing myself say, "Yes, Father." It is hard not to. Forward and back. All of a sudden he stops moving and turns toward me. I feel my body stiffen. He is staring hard. I draw back a little in the chair. Then abruptly he turns away again with a sound like a growl. When he speaks the words are not for me. "Death is a fifty-fifty thing, maybe forty-forty," he says in a flat voice.

I watch the sentence come clawing into me like a lost tribe. That's the way it is with dementia. There are a number of simple questions I could ask. Like, Father what do you mean? Or, Father what about the other twenty percent? Or, Father tell me what you were thinking all those years when we sat at the kitchen table together munching cold bacon and listening to each other's silence? I can still hear the sound of the kitchen clock ticking on the wall above the table. "Yes," I say.

When my father began to lose his mind, my mother and I simply pretended otherwise. You can get used to eating breakfast with a man in a fedora. You can get used to anything, my mother was in the habit of saying. I began to wake earlier and earlier in the morning. I would come back in from my morning walk about dawn, to find him standing in his pajamas and his hat, whispering, "Supper ready yet?" to the dark kitchen, his face clear as a child's. This was before confusion gave way to rages. Dementia can be gleeful at first. One evening I was making salad when he came through the kitchen. "The letters of your lettuce are very large," he said quietly and kept going. A deep chuckle floated back. Other days I saw him sitting with his head sunk in his hands. I left the room. Late at night I could hear him in the room next to mine, walking up and down, saying something over and over. He was cursing himself. The sound came through the wall. A sound not human. That night I dreamed I was given abdominal surgery with a coat hanger. I bought earplugs for sleeping.

But I was learning the most important thing there is to learn about dementia, that it is continuous with sanity. There is no door that slams shut suddenly. Father had always been a private man. Now his mind was a sacred area where no one could enter or ask the way. Father had always been a bit irascible. Now his moods were a minefield where we stepped carefully, holding out one hand horizontally before us. Father had always disliked disorder. Now he spent all day bent over scraps of paper, writing notes to himself which he hid in books or his clothing and at once forgot. We did not try to keep track of them, this angered him the more. "I can feel summer sinking into the earth," my mother said one evening. We were sitting in the back garden. He had asked what time it was and gone in to write that down. She told him six o'clock, although it was only five, hoping he would spend about an hour writing 6 on pieces of paper and then realize six o'clock is suppertime and come to the table without trouble. To live with a mad person requires many small acts of genius—reverse of the moment when Helen Keller shouts "Water!"—when you glance into the mad world and suddenly see how it works. My mother got good at this. I did not. I became interested in penance.

Let us be gentle when we question our fathers.

It wasn't until he went mad that I began to see I had always angered him. I never knew why. I did not ask. Instead I had learned to take soundings—like someone testing the depth of a well. You throw a stone down and listen. You wait for the gaps and say, "Yes."

I was a locked person. I had hit the wall. Something had to break. I wrote a poem called "I Am an Unlocated Window of Myself" (which my father found on the kitchen table and covered with the words GARBAGE DAY FRIDAY written in pencil forty or fifty times). I prayed and fasted. I read the mystics. I studied the martyrs. I began to think I was someone thirsting for God. And then I met a man who told me about the pilgrimage to Compostela.

He was a pious man who knew how to ask questions. "How can you see your life unless you leave it?" he said to me. Penance began to look more interesting. Since ancient times pilgrimages have been conducted from place to place, in the belief that a question can travel into an answer as water into thirst. The most venerable pilgrimage in Christendom is called the Road to Compostela—some 850 kilometers of hills and stars and desert from St. Jean Pied de Port on the French side of the Pyrenees to the city of Compostela on the western coast of the Spanish province of Galicia. Pilgrims have walked this road since the ninth century. They say the holy apostle James lies buried in Compostela and that he admires being visited. In fact, it is traditional for pilgrims to take a petition to Compostela; you can ask St. James to change your life. I was a young, strong, stingy person of no particular gender—all traits advantageous to the pilgrim. So I set off, into the late spring wind blasting with its green states.

To look for the simplest question, the most obvious facts, the doors that no one may close, is what I meant by anthropology. I was 'a strong soul. Look I will change everything, all the meanings! I thought. I packed my rucksack with socks, canteen, pencils, three empty notebooks. I took no maps, I cannot read maps—why press a seal on running water? After all, the only rule of travel is, Don't come back the way you went. Come a new way.

Kinds of Water:
An Essay on the Road to Compostela

St. Jean Pied de Port   *20th of June*

> *the good thing is we know*
> *the glasses are for drinking*
>
> Machado

At the foot of the port of Roncesvalles, a small town bathes itself. Thunderstorms come down from the mountains at evening. Balls of fire roll through the town. Air cracks apart like a green fruit. Underneath my hotel window is a river (La Nive) with a sizable waterfall. There is a dark shape at the edge of the falls, as I look down, knocking this way and that in the force of the current. It would seem to be a drowned dog. It is a drowned dog. And I stand, mind burning, looking down. No one is noticing the dog. Should I mention it? I do not know the word for *drowned*. Am I on the verge of an ancient gaffe? Waiters come and go on the terrace of the hotel bar, bending deeply from the waist to serve potage. A fathom below them the dark body slaps. At the foot of the falls, where water is rushing away, a fisherman casts his line over it. What sense could there be in things? I have come through countries, centuries of difficult sleep and hard riding and still I do not know the sense of things when I see it, when I stand with the pieces in my hands. Could there be a sculpture of a drowned dog on the ledge of an ancient waterfall? I watch and pass, hours pass. My mind a laughingstock. Evening falls, the shape is still there. Fisherman gone, waiters whisking tablecloths on the terrace. What is it others know?

Pilgrims were people who loved a good riddle.

From St. Jean Pied de Port   *21st of June*

> Presently, to a distant tinkling of bells, they turned and
> started off. The retreating figures made Kan-ami think of a
> line from the pilgrim's canticle they had practiced so ear-
> nestly with the innkeeper the evening before:
>
>> Hopefully we take the path from afar
>> to the temple where blooms
>> the flower of the good law.
>
>   *Tanizaki*

It rained during the night. We sit on the hotel terrace drinking
coffee. Morning sparkles on us. I watch the dog. One soaked
paw has moved over the ledge and is waving back and forth
as water streams around it. The man I am traveling with peers
vaguely toward it: "Ah!" and returns to eating bread. His
concern is with the more historical aspects of pilgrimage. Pil-
grims, for example, were traditionally gracious people and
wore wide-brimmed hats in order that they might doff them
to other pilgrims. The man I am traveling with demonstrates
how this should be done. I think I will call him "My Cid." It
speeds up the storytelling. Besides, he is one "who in a happy
hour was born," as the famous poem says. You will see this as
the journey proceeds, see him sailing through danger and smil-
ing at wounds. Perhaps I—no, he is waiting for me. I doff my

hat in the general direction of the waterfall, and we set off. Behold now this good fortune.

By afternoon it is darker, thunder comes down the hills. Presently we are in Spain. In the bar where we stop, a press of people, a small cup of coffee. I wipe the table with my hat: paws still dripping.

When is a pilgrim like a sieve? When he riddles.

Buergete   *22nd of June*

> unmoved the melons
> don't seem to recall
> a drop
> of last night's downpour
>
>   Sodo

The small hotel of Buergete is made of water. Outside, rain streams all night. Roofs pour, the gutters float with frogs and snails. You would not see me—I lie in the dark listening, swirling. Walls of the hotel are filled with water. Plumbing booms and sluices. A water clock, embedded in the heart of the building, measures out our hours in huge drops. Wheels and gears turn in the walls, the roaring of lovers washes over the ceiling, the staircase is an aqueduct of cries. From below I can hear a man dreaming. A deep ravine goes down to the sea, he calls out, rushes over the edge. The mechanisms that keep us from drowning are so fragile: and why us?

In the morning the hotel is dark, no sign of life, no smell of coffee. Old clock ticking in the deserted hall. Dining room empty, shutters drawn, napkins in glasses. Morning drifts on. I peer into the kitchen: still as a church. Everyone has been washed away in the night. We pile money on the table in the hall, leave without breakfast, without ado! as they say in my country. Outside is silent, street dissolving, far hills running down in streaks. We filter westward.

Pilgrims were people who figured things out as they walked. On the road you can think forward, you can think back, you can make a list to remember to tell those at home.

To Pamplona   23rd of June

> When he thought of the fragile O-hisa made over to look
> like the winsome pilgrim of the Kabuki and of the old man
> at her side ringing a pilgrim's bell and intoning a canticle
> from one holy place to the next, Kan-ami could not help
> feeling a little envious. The old man chose his pleasures
> well. Kan-ami had heard that it was not uncommon for men
> of taste in Osaka to dress a favourite geisha as a pilgrim and
> do the Awaji circuit with her every year. The old man, much
> taken with the idea, announced that he would make this the
> first of an annual series. Always afraid of sunburn, O-hisa
> was less enthusiastic. "How does it go? We sleep at Hachi-
> kenya, is it? Where do you suppose Hachikenya is?"
>
> Tanizaki

Kinds of water drown us. Kinds of water do not. My water jar
splashes companiably on my back as I walk. A pool of
thoughts tilts this way and that in me. Sokrates, after bathing,
came back to his cell unhurriedly and drank the hemlock. The
others wept. Swans swam in around him. And he began to talk
about the coming journey, to an unknown place far from their
tears, which he did not understand. People really understand
very little of one another. Sometimes when I speak to him, My
Cid looks very hard and straight into my face as if in search of
something (a city on a map?) like someone who has tumbled

off a star. But he is not the one who feels alien—ever, I think. He lives in a small country of hope, which is his heart. Like Sokrates he fails to understand why travel should be such a challenge to the muscles of the heart, for other people. Around every bend of the road is a city of gold, isn't it?

I am the kind of person who thinks no, probably not. And we walk, side by side, in different countries.

Pilgrims were people in scientific exile.

Puente la Reina   *24th of June*

> *the world so unsure, unknowable*
> *the world so unsure, unknowable*
> *who knows—our griefs may*
> *hold our greatest hopes.*

> *Zeami*

A bridge is a meeting point, where those who started out—
how many, now how many nights ago?—come together.
Hearts uneasy in their depths. It was in the medieval city of
Puente la Reina that all the pilgrims heading for Compostela,
from France and Spain and Italy and other points of origin,
met at the crossing of the River Arga. Except, in those days,
there was no crossing. Boatmen plied the river—many of them
not honest men at all, but sordid assassins who took advantage
of the pilgrims! Kinds of water drown us. Evil boatmen threw
many a pilgrim to his watery death. Then an act of grace
supervened. The queen of Spain was moved to pity for the
pilgrims' difficult situation. She gave it some thought. How
could she defend them? Why not a bridge! A beautiful, antic,
keyholed construction, washed by gold shadows on the under-
side (photograph). She smiled, when she saw it, out of the side
of her eyes: CURVA PELIGROSA says the sign on the bridge to
this day. Deadly slant. There were stars in the plane trees and
stars in her eyes. There were pilgrims singing on the bridge.

There were boatmen who turned to worse crime. Such is the balance of human efforts.

Pilgrims were people wondering, wondering. Whom shall I meet now?

Estella   *25th of June*

> *like lame-wheeled carriages*
> *we creep forth reluctantly*
> *on the journey from the capital*
>
>   *Zeami*

On dark mornings in Navarre the fall-off hills rise in masses, flat on top. White clouds bite down on them like teeth. In my country too it is morning now, they are making coffee, they are getting out the black bread. No one eats black bread here. Spanish bread is the same color as the stones that lie along the roadside—gold. True, I often mistake stones for bread. Pilgrims' hunger is a curious thing.

The road itself was built by the pilgrims of ancient times as they walked. Each carried a stone and set it in place. As is clear from the photographs, these were in general stones of quite good size. While the pilgrims trudged, they would pretend the stones were loaves of bread and, to keep spirits high, they sang songs about bread, or about the rock that was following them. *¡No me mates con tomate, mátame con bacalao!* You can hear this one still, in bars, some nights. Don't kill me with tomato, kill me with cod! What is it that keeps us from drowning in moments that rise and cover the heart?

Pilgrims were people whose recipes were simple.

To Nájera   *27th of June*

> *we pick spring greens*
> *in the little field of Ikuta*
> *a sight so charming*
> *the traveler stops to watch*
> *foolishness! all these questions*
>
>   *Kan-ami*

Rain during the night. No guests in the hotel except My Cid and me. Yet, just before dawn, someone made his way down the stairs and past our rooms to the bath. Much noise of taps and other facilities. A rough cough. I fell asleep, when I woke he was gone. In the plaza we find bars and shops already open, how surprising. We purchase blood oranges and eat them very fast. It is already late when you wake up inside a question. Rose petals are being swept from the church steps as we pass, and faces in the doorway are lit with vague regret. Someone has roused the town, not me. Someone has been gained and lost, someone of value. Are there two ways of knowing the world—a submissive and a devouring way? They end up roughly the same place.

Pilgrims were people who tried not to annoy the regular inhabitants.

Nájera   *28th of June*

> 'moon drifts in cloud
> I have a mind
> to borrow
> a small ripe melon
>
>   Shiki

We are moving on the edge of the Meseta. Hills are harsher, terraced, red soil shows through the green like sunburn. Small trees line up in spikes on the horizon. No more deep woods shaded for battle. No more long winds rolling down from Roland's eyes.

You see that uncertainty along the horizon (photograph)? Not rain. It is heat haze on the plain of León.

Water is less, and less.

In Nájera are buried the kings of Navarre. They lie on their tombs long-limbed and cool as water plants. The stone faces are full of faith but rather private, with a characteristic set to the lips: one straight incision across like the first cut made by a man peeling his orange with a knife. My Cid, as you know, prefers the speckled kind called blood oranges, which are quick to eat but slow to peel. Cleaning his knives reminds him of a story. There was once a pilgrim who carried a turnip all the way from France. A turnip of quite good size. He had in mind to feast his fellow pilgrims on the last hill outside Compostela and be king of their hearts for a while. Thieves broke his head open just as he came to the top of the hill. The good man's name has not come down to us, but the hill is still there and is called Monte del Gozo. From where you are perhaps you can see it. Mountain of Joy. My Cid tells these old stories wonderfully well. He has two knives, for different sizes of oranges.

Pilgrims were people who carried knives but rarely found use for them.

Santo Domingo de la Calzada   *29th of June*

> *waited for you along the road, I did—*
> *silent, silent, walking alone*
> *but today again the darkness falls*

> *Gensei*

As we move into Castile we are accompanied on either side of
the road by aqueducts and other more modern systems of
irrigation, for the water grows less. Like pastries of red lava
the rocks rise in visible layers. Fields are no longer dark and
edged close with woods but stretch out and roll away beneath
the eye, sectioned in areas of ocher and amber and red. Nine
months of winter, three months of hell is the proverbial de-
scription of climate on the Meseta. No dark green wheat riding
in waves under the wind here, as there was all through Na-
varre. No wind at all. That smell is light, ready to fall on us.
One day closer to the plain of León.

We live by waters breaking out of the heart.

My Cid loves heat and is very elated. He rarely gets thirsty.
"I was born in the desert." Twice a day, at meals, he drinks a
lot of wine, staring at the glass in genial amazement as it
empties itself again and again. He grows heavier and heavier
like a piece of bread soaking, or a fish that floats dreamily out
of my fingers down deeper and deeper in the tank, turning
round now and then to make dim motions at me with its fins,
as if in recognition, but in fact it does not recognize me—gold

shadows flash over it, out of reach, gone. Who is this man? I have no idea. The more I watch him, the less I know. What are we doing here, and why are our hearts invisible? Once last winter when we were mapping out the pilgrimage on his kitchen table, he said to me, "Well, what are you afraid of, then?" I said nothing. "Nothing." Not an answer. What would your answer be?

We think we live by keeping water caught in the trap of the heart. *Coger en un trampa* is a Spanish idiom meaning "to catch in a trap." *Coger por el buen camino* is another, constructed with the same verb; it means "to get the right road." And yet to ensnare is not necessarily to take the right road.

Afraid I don't love you enough to do this.

Pilgrims were people who got the right verb.

Villa Major del Río   *30th of June*

> As I look back over the many years of my frivolous life, I
> remember at one time I coveted an official post with a tenure
> of land and at another time I was anxious to confine myself
> within the walls of a monastery. Yet I kept aimlessly wan-
> dering on like a cloud in the wind . . . it is because I believe
> there is no place in this world that is not an unreal dwelling.
> At this point I abandoned the line of thinking and went to
> sleep.
>
>   *Basho*

The town of Villa Major del Río, My Cid observes, is three
ways a lie. "It is not a town, it is not big and there is no river."
The observations are correct. Notwithstanding, we lunch, and
over lunch a conversation—about action, in which he does
not believe. I would relate the conversation and outline the
theory of his belief but theories elude me unless I write them
down at the time. Instead, I was watching his dreamy half
smile. It floats up through his face from the inside, like water
filling an aquarium, when he talks about God. For his conver-
sations about action (we have had more than one) are all de-
scriptions of God, deep nervous lover's descriptions.

I should have taken photographs. A theory of action is
hard to catch, and I know only glimpses of his life—for in-
stance, at home he makes his own bread (on Saturday morn-

ing, very good bread). He thought about being a priest (at one time). He could have made a career on the concert stage, and instead built a harpsichord (red) in the dining room. The harpsichord goes unmentioned in Villa Major del Río. I am telling you this because a conversation is a journey, and what gives it value is fear. You come to understand travel because you have had conversations, not vice versa. What is the fear inside language? No accident of the body can make it stop burning.

To Burgos   *2nd of July*

> *what does he do—*
> *the man next door*
> *in the abode in late autumn?*

> *Basho*

"The land is lean indeed!" He quotes from the poem as we
begin our long, cold climb up the windswept plateau of
Burgos. Cold is the mountain road that goes curving up. Cold
are the woods where winds come roaring out at us as if we
were enemies—or birds, for here are tiny birds walking about
on the road, who have strolled out of their homes in the tree-
tops now level with the road as we ascend—and there is no
one else. The wind is too loud to talk. He walks ahead, eyes
front.

   In the city of Burgos lies El Cid himself—beside Ximena
he rests in an eternal conversation. Beneath the transept of
Burgos Cathedral they have lain since 1921, and before that,
in a burial place in the city from the year 1835, and previously,
seven hundred years in the monastery of San Pedro outside
the city walls. By now, she must know every word he is going
to say. Yet she kisses his mouth and the eyes of his face, she
kisses his hands, his truth, his marrow. What is the conversa-
tion of lovers? Compared with ordinary talk, it is as bread to
stones. My heart gets dizzy. It is the most difficult photograph
I have tried to take so far: up the scaffolding, hand over hand
and out onto the pinnacles they blow, her hair like a red sail

as they veer around storks' nests in the wind and clutch wide at the railings, leaning out over the tiny city, its clockwork shadows so crazily far below. One shriek goes flaring and flattening away down the valley. Gone. She kisses him on the shoulder in the Moorish custom. They look at one another. They look into the light. They jump.

There is no question I covet that conversation. There is no question I am someone starving. There is no question I am making this journey to find out what that appetite is. And I see him free of it, as if he had simply crossed to the other side of a bridge, I see desire set free in him like some ray of mysterious light. Now tell me the truth, would you cross that bridge if you came to it? And where, if you made the grave choice to give up bread, would it take you? You see what I fear. One night I dreamed of such a world. I rowed upon the surface of the Moon and there was no wind, there were no moments, for the Moon is as empty as the inside of an eye and not even the sound of a shadow falling falls there. I know you want me to tell you that hunger and silence can lead you to God, so I will say it, but I awoke. As the nail is parted from the flesh, I awoke and I was alone.

Ahead of me walks a man who knows the things I want to know about bread, about God, about lovers' conversations, yet mile after tapping mile goes by while I watch his heels rise and fall in front of me and plant my feet in rhythm to his pilgrim's staff as it strikes the road, white dust puffing up to cover each step, left, right, left.

When is a pilgrim like a letter of the alphabet? When he cries out.

From Burgos   3rd of July

> now I return to the burning house
> but where is the place I used to live?
>
> Kan-ami

Cold Burgos is beautiful to leave along the avenue of dark
plane trees that line the river. Whiteness floats on the water.
At the bend of the river a waterbird stands on one long, chill
leg. He turns an eye. *Adios.* Gladly and bravely we go—how
surprising. Burgos was to have been for us a major interval,
some four days of luxury and recuperation, according to our
original itinerary. Instead, we stay just long enough to mend
our trousers and tie new straps on our hats. The cloud-moving
wind calls through our sleep: we rise too early, look at one
another, set off again. It is an open secret among pilgrims
and other theoreticians of this traveling life that you become
addicted to the horizon. There is a momentum of walking,
hunger, roads, empty bowl of thoughts that is more luxurious
—more civil than any city. Even the earliest *Pilgrim's Guide,*
published in A.D. 1130, contains remarks touching the di-
lemma of the pilgrim who reaches his destination and cannot
bear to stop. But that is not my question, presently.

My questions, as you know, concern pilgrims' tradition.
Animals ride on top of one another. Animals ensnare them-
selves in plants and tendrils. These are two motifs that may be

seen repeatedly in reliefs and other works of art along the pilgrims' route. Signs are given to us like a voice within flesh, that is my question. Signs point our virtue. I want to ask how is it this man and I are riding on top of one another, and how ensnared, for it is not in the customary ways. We take separate rooms in hotels. Carnal interest is absent. Yet tendrils are not. A pilgrim is a person who is up to something. What is it? A pilgrim is a person who works out an attitude to tendrils and other things that trammel the feet, what should that be? Chop them as fast as they grow with my sharp pilgrim's knife? Or cherish them, hoarding drops of water of every kind to aid their struggle? Love is the mystery inside this walking. It runs ahead of us on the road like a dog, out of the photograph.

To Castrogeriz   *4th of July*

> *twisting up hemp*
> *I spin a thread that has no use*
> *the tears that fall*
> *are not beads for stringing*
>
>   *Tsurayuki*

We walk for hours through a single wheat field stretching as far as the eye can see in every direction to the sky. Hills come lower. Horizon flattens. Color begins to bleach out of the landscape as we move onto the Meseta. No more red clay. Where soil shows through the vegetation now it is white, or the porous gray of pumice, and powders off in the wind. Trees are short and clenched like fists in a Goya painting. No rivers at all today until just outside the town of Castrogeriz we cross the Río Odra, a dry gulley.

My Cid has taken to wearing a goatskin bag (*odra*) for carrying water. He is rarely thirsty but likes the effect of it slung across his body like a gangster's gun, and he is perfecting the knack of shooting water from the goatskin into his mouth with one hand while reading a map in the other as he walks. Half smile. Very ordinary behavior can be striking when it plays in the shapes of things like a sage, or a child biting into a pear. In the photograph the two of us are bending over the map, looking for Castrogeriz which has been obscured by water drops. Here is an enlargement. You can see, within each drop, a horizon stretching, hard, in full wind. Enlarged further, faint dark shapes become visible, gathering on the edge of the plain of León.

¡Corazón arriba!

Castrogeriz   *4th of July*

> *I will gaze at the moon*
> *and cleanse my heart*
>
> *Zeami*

Castrogeriz is a pile of history. It is layered upward from the dry ravine of the Odra to the ancient remains of a Roman camp high on top of the rock. This smashed Roman grin commands the rock and the town and the whole valley below. It stands behind every sound, like something dripping.

Why then I wonder, in the town of Castrogeriz, do they turn the water off at night? Not only in each house but in the fountain of the central square and also in all the fountains of the lesser plazas. A surprise, and a long dry night for me. I walk back to the hotel, hands hanging down. Surprises make a child of us: here is another. A moon rising, edge so sharp you can feel it in your back teeth. By the time she is full, there will be two grave children walking the plain of León. Unexpectedness moves us along. And the moon—so perfectly charted—never fails to surprise us. I wonder why. The moon makes a traveler hunger for something bitter in the world, what is it? I will vanish; others will come here, what is that? An old question.

Well, a pilgrim is like a No play. Each one has the same structure, a question mark.

To Frómista   *5th of July*

> *daybreak comes on distinctly*
> *with sounds of a punted boat*
> *does not the dissolving moon*
> *stay yet in the sky?*

                                    Shohaku

Every morning as I walk behind him, I gather a handful of
flowers which My Cid pins to his hat. Flowers are banal be-
tween lovers but this is not that. Mine are much less an offer-
ing to My Cid than an entangling of him in an offering to the
saint, which is in turn an entangling of the saint in an offering
to God, as the pin snares the flower stalks and the hat gives
occasion to the whole. As you know from the photographs,
Saint James in his day was insouciance itself—with his great
hat tilted low over one eye and his blue cloak unfurling around
him like the first notes of paradise. Morning is clear. The
hearths smoke. Distances go silent.

Pilgrims were debonair people.

Frómista   *7th of July*

> *as one turns about the moon*
> *understands one's very heart*
>
> *Sozei*

Hills continue to pale and scarify. They look shaved, like old heads of women in an asylum. What is the breaking point of the average pilgrim? I feel so lonely, like childhood again. What kind of ensnaring can touch the loneliness of animals? Nothing can touch it. No, maybe that is not altogether correct. This evening My Cid gave me a back rub and spoke to me, more kindly than he has before, about his mother, who suffers from a wasting disease. Once, when he first learned of her illness, his heart broke. Then he set about taking care of her, with back rubs and other attentions. A voice coming from behind your back can be different. Animals who ride on top of one another do not have to see one another's face. Sometimes that is better.

Carrión de los Condes   *7th of July*

> *as usual with men who are blind*
> *my ears are sharp, you know*
> *you just called me "a man without feelings"*
> *don't go on saying things like that!*
>
> *Zeami*

The morning is clear. The morning is immensely clear. Lower
the lance and lean forward in the saddle. It is time to question
him about the loneliness. His answer both surprises me and
does not.

He has not been lonely since he was thirty, when he took
the decision to channel his sadness into forms "more meta-
physical." He began to think about penance. Like a blind poet
of ancient times, he built his hut on a meeting slope, chose a
small number of objects and waited for friends. Fish dart out
of gold regions. His loves are deep, sudden services. And his
delight is of a very particular kind. "You have a passion for
people who are pelted, Dan," says Sir Hugo to Daniel De-
ronda in a novel I read once. My Cid lives this novel; his
friends are ones in affliction. She is someone who has known
hardship, he often begins. Has a bad back, father abandoned
her, gives all her money away to the poor, history of lunacy,
lost the whole family, royalty—fallen, nowhere to go. He loves
these stories—they make people seem real. Nonetheless there

are difficulties. People mistake his intentions, especially women, and some do drown.

For women may regard a story as the beginning of something, like a love affair. Serious mistake. For him it is already the end: *Se abandona*. Persons studying the photographs from different angles may see different tendrils, but for him these entanglements are not a problem. It is you who are lonely.

And in the end, his tendency to rescue maidens is not something I can explain to you, or dramatize—I am a pilgrim (not a novelist) and the only story I have to tell is the road itself. Besides, no one can write a novel about a road, any more than you can write a novel about God, simply because you cannot get around the back of it. A round character is one you can see around. He changes according to the company he keeps. He moves but your movements are always larger, and circumnavigate his. Inside the minds of other characters you can see him flicker past, suddenly funny—or evil. Now I think it is true to say of the road, and also of God, that it does not move. At the same time, it is everywhere. It has a language, but not one I know. It has a story, but I am in it. So are you. And to realize this is a moment of some sadness. When we are denied a story, a light goes off—Daniel Deronda vanishes: do we vanish too? I am asking you to study the dark.

Sahagún   *8th of July*

> *no wind, yet the windbells*
> *keep on ringing*
>
> *Shiren*

The light is astounding, a hammer. Horizon no closer, ever.
Hills again change color: gold and dark gold and darker gold.
Whole fields are nothing but slabs of this gold soil, smashed
up in chunks for cultivation, as if the massive altar at Castro-
geriz had toppled straight across León. The pieces of bread
that line the pilgrims' road have the color and shape of the
round loaves of León, many show bites taken out. They were
famished people who built this road.

My Cid and I have our first open anger today. It cut like
glass. Animals entangle themselves in one another, and grow
enraged. (What is rage?)

When I spoke to him about the loneliness, I didn't mean
out in the wheat fields. There is a loneliness that opens up
between two people sitting in a bar, not in love with each
other, not even certain they like the way they are entangled
with each other, one taps a glass with a spoon, stops. There is
a silence that pounds down on two people. More astounding
than the light that hammers the plain of León, at least for
those animals who choose to fear it. (Is it a choice?)

El Burgo Ranero   *9th of July*

> *your autumn leaves—*
> *it is because they fall we love them*
> *so why not launch our Takase river boat?*
>
>   *Shikibu*

It would be an almost perfect love affair, wouldn't it? that between the pilgrim and the road. No mistake, it is a beautiful thing, the *camino*. It stretches away from you. It leads to real gold: Look at the way it shines. And it asks only one thing. Which happens to be the one thing you long to give. You step forward. You shiver in the light. Nothing is left in you but desire for that perfect economy of action, using up the whole heart, no residue, no mistake: *camino*. It would be as simple as water, wouldn't it? If there were any such thing as simple action for animals like us.

Pilgrims were people glad to take off their clothing, which was on fire.

Mansilla de las Mulas   *10th of July*

> bones on the moor
> wind blows on them through my heart
>
>   Basho

Meseta colder than expected. Distances crushing. Horizon beats on the eyes.

Everything is gold. I cannot describe the gold. I have shown you the photographs (or have I?) but they don't come near it. You get almost no warning. Something is coming along the edge of the wheat, drumming the plain like a horseman, you stop, listen, begin to turn—don't!

It is life taken over; *esa es la verdad*.

To León   *11th of July*

> *the rumour is already*
> *in circulation*
> *yet when I began to love*
> *there was not a soul who knew*
>
> *Tadamine*

Water abandons itself. Gold does not. Gold takes life over.

There are drownings on the Meseta. I will show you the photographs if you like but, really, in this case they are not helpful. Because the light is not something you see, exactly. You don't look at it, or breathe, you feel a pressure but you don't look. It is like being in the same room as a man you love. Other people are in the room. He may be smoking a cigarette. And you know you are not strong enough to look at him (yet) although the fact that he is there, silent and absent beside a thin wisp of cigarette smoke, hammers you. You rest your chin on your hand, like a saint on a pillar. Moments elongate and drop. A radiance is hitting your skin from somewhere, every nerve begins to burn outward through the surface, your lungs float in a substance like rage, sweet as rage, no!—don't look. Something falling from your mouth like bits of rust.

Well, the photograph—after all it may give some idea of the thing. From outside it all, looking down: two tiny figures moving on the Meseta. Two animals enraged with each other. How can you tell? Pay particular attention to the nerves. Every one is visible. See, as they burn, you can look right down the heart's core. See it crumble like old dry bread.

To León 11th of July

> *In the No play* Obasute, *at the line "I feel ashamed to see
> the moon," there exists a moment when the acting can be
> so effective that (as they say) "gold is picked up in the
> middle of the road."*
>
> *Zeami*

A baking hot morning. I can feel you watching. I shrug and
go on.

In allegorical renderings of the pilgrimage to Compostela,
days spent crossing the plain of León stand for the dark night
of the soul—how can it help being that way? Although we
taste everything and take on every animal, although your true
love exists (and maybe it does), we continue to behave more
or less like the people we are, even on a pilgrimage. No soul
ever goes dark enough for you. Look again at the photograph.
Two figures moving on the Meseta, running slowly on a table
of gold. Running with arms out, mouths open. Two small
ensnared animals howling toward Finisterre.

You can lead a pilgrim to water.

León   *12th of July*

> *when in the clear water*
> *at Ausaka border*
> *it sees its reflection*
> *the tribute horse from Mochizuki*
> *will surely shy away*
>
> *Zeami*

Various dangers come at you from water. We cross the top of
the world and descend into the city of León in conditions
much different than expected. Lashing rain and slate gray
winds, horizontal and cold as winter. Something is being pre-
pared on the plain of León. The city itself is a bright animal,
bustling, turning, restless to lie down. We find lodgings and
fall asleep. Storms pass over the city. My Cid dreams of levia-
thans coming up out of the water to kill him. He impales one
of them on his pilgrim's staff and hurls it back, losing his staff
(I point out). But the creature will (he feels sure) be purified
on its journey downstream to the ends of the earth. A clean
gold animal clambering ashore at the end of the world, isn't
that so? I am the kind of person who says let's wait and see.

Arzóa   *12th of July*

> *she at once capped his verses*
>
> *Shikibu*

My Cid and I are very polite with each other. At the same time, somewhat dialectical—that is, I contradict everything he says. I have been trying to curb this habit by picking up pieces of bread from along the roadside to gnaw as I walk. It must have been, in origin, for this purpose that pilgrims began to put the bread there.

An origin is not an action, although it occurs (perhaps loudly) at the very start and may open an action (as in breaking a gun). How long ago it seems we started out. In the photographs from this leg of the journey you will notice a certain absence of scale clues, so that a bullet-pocked rock seems to hold the heavens.

Pilgrims were people who took a surprisingly long time to cross the head of a pin.

Orbigo   *13th of July*

> since my house burned down
> I now own
> a better view
> of the rising moon

> Masahide

Color begins to return to the fields as we move toward the edge of the Meseta. There are green potato fields cut by canals. Avenues of poplar trees turn their bright soles to the wind. Horizon closing in. Behind the light, toward the west, (darkish) shadows are gathering. That would be animals on the rim of the plain. That would be the wolf.

The pieces of bread along the roadside are blacker now and more wildly bitten. At the same time, in some places you see whole loaves thrown down untouched. Curious. Insouciance may escalate to proportions of madness at this stage in the pilgrimage. Breaking points appear.

Astorga   *14th of July*

> the dried sardine is broiled at noon
> but in this back country
> the use of coins is not yet heard of
> what a bother to travellers
>
>   *Basho*

Those things that cut across the time are what you remember,
voices cutting across sleep.

"*¡Agua! ¡Agua!*" ripping through my siesta like a color.

Red. The color red speeds through the land as we move
into the mountains again. Sections of brick red soil mark out
the green plantings of the hills as they rise. Poppies flash along
the roadside, amid dark chunks of rusted bread. At noon, the
cicadas let their red throats crack open. Red, My Cid informs
me, is the only color wolves see: this is taken as clear testi-
mony, in ancient Celt-Iberian belief, that they are genuinely
royal animals.

It is over lunch that we talk of wolves, and My Cid has
ordered trout. The scales and eyes are gold as it sizzles on the
plate. He cuts in. The flesh is a deep rose color. After lunch,
we proceed to the museum to see a twelfth-century statue
called *The Virgin of the Trout,* with wooden cheeks of the
same rose color. Her smile an underwater bell. Ancient pil-
grims traveled from far and wide, on delicately tinted feet, to
visit her. And there is still more red, as we move from the

museum to the cathedral, for the cathedral at Astorga wears a deep blush. Its porch of rose limestone is inscribed with scenes of shame: Christ expelling moneylenders from the temple, and others. Now we are close to the heart of the color. Shame. Look at the photograph. Yes, it is a picture of a hole in a wall.

The hole dates from medieval times. It is located in the west wall of the cathedral at a height of about two meters above the head of My Cid. Behind it is a pit opening into the wall and, in front, iron bars. Women once placed themselves inside the pit and lived there, taking as sustenance only what was offered by those passing by. Many a pilgrim on his way to Compostela shared his meager rations with the women, handing in water or pieces of bread or whatever he had. Others passed with their eyes on the road. Some tossed stones through the bars. It is a strange economy that shame sets up, isn't it? Almost as strange as that of honor. Pilgrims blush in broad daylight. Women blush in a hole. They trade morsels of gold through a grillwork and so all live to overcome another day. What is a blush?

Dum pudeo pereo ("as I blush, I die"), says an old love song. Blood rushes to the face, at the same time the heart seems to wither in on itself and snap, like the eye socket of a trout when it hits the hot oil. Shame is the presence of someone right up against me. Hot because her eyes are closer to me than my own honor. She is a woman in a pit in a wall with a stone hot as the midday sun in her hands: listen, footsteps go fading down the street. She is My Cid cut open by a word from me, him weeping within me. Kinds of water drown us.

The women in the wall were called *las emparedadas* ("the

walled-in ones"). What is a pilgrim's life after he quits the *camino?* There is an ancient tradition: the afterlife of a pilgrim is three ways shame. Never hungry again. He will eat and eat and taste nothing. Never free again, according to the terms of the freedom he finds while bound to the road. Never angry again, with that kind of rage that scorches two animals ensnared on the Meseta. It is an anger hard to come back from as death, or so it seems to me now as I recollect the day near Sahagún when My Cid and I cut ourselves open on a moment of anger and blasphemed your name. Let's take out those photographs again, *momentito.* There is something here that deserves to be studied, there is a sense of the excitement and danger of the night. And yet it was broad day: look.

from today the dew
will erase the inscription on my hat
"I am one of two travelling together"

Basho

I have never felt life to be as slow and desperate as that day on the Meseta with the sky empty above us, hour after hour unmoving before us and a little wind whistling along the bone of my ear. Walking across the top of the world. Hours give no shade. Wind gives no shade.

Sky does not move. Sky crushes all that moves.

We had been out since sunrise, we were growing black. Then we saw water.

A plane tree in the middle of the desert with a spring beside it. We ran to it and drank, drank more, grew arrogant. Here I am swaggering like a torero around the little oasis, or so it looks (photograph) water all over my face. Now I ask My Cid a question—and what follows—well, it may seem to be nothing at all. But in fact it was sackcloth of hair and the moon became blood. He begins to answer the question (I don't remember what it was). And he has a certain way of answering a question (as we all do). And I know what he is going to say (as soon as he begins). And all at once I am enraged. My sharp pilgrim's knife flashes once. "I know!" right across his open face.

I know. I know what you say. I know who you are. I know all that you mean. Why does it enrage an animal to be given what it already knows? Speaking as someone who is as much in love with knowledge as My Cid is in love with the light on the plain of León, I would say that knowing is a road. The metaphor is unoriginal but now you may set it beside the photographs of the pit in the wall and see what it signifies to me.

You reach out your hand for bread and grasp a stone. You touch stone, you feel sweat running down your body. Sweat running, day going black, it is a moment that does not move. How I did waste and exhaust my heart. Something darker appears to be running down the body of the saint in the photograph, but it is just an effect of the light filter we were using on the Meseta. There is nothing darker (than the second death).

Now that I study them, however, I have to confess the photographs of the *emparedadas* are something of an embarrassment. I tried to angle my lens so as to shoot through the bars but the grillwork was too high. None of them printed properly. Look at this one, for instance—it could be a picture of a woman with something in her hands. It could be a drowned dog floating in bits of stone. Can you make it out? The picture has been taken looking directly into the light, a fundamental error. As I was considering these matters, he had gone his way, footsteps fading down the street like the last drops of water running out of a basin. I hurry after him. Kinds of water drown us. Kinds of water blister the negatives irremediably (prints look burned). Perhaps I will have time to put these through again later.

Molinaseca   *16th of July*

> *voice of wind in pines*
> *makes the solitude familiar*
> *who will do such waking for each dawn?*
>
> *Sogi*

Mountains: We have come over the mountains of León. It takes a whole day from light to light. The road goes winding, winding, winding up. The road goes plunging down. You understand these were words before: *up, down.* It is nearly my limit, nearly stupor, whereas he grows lighter and lighter as he walks. What is penance?

Up.

On top of the mountains of León is an iron cross. Here we stop. A wind whistles up one side of the mountains from early times, mornings, much too far away and still those mornings, down on the plain of León. "Somewhere down there we were hot," he says. Somewhere down there we were drowning. I fall over on a flat rock and fall asleep, while he watches. Wolves come and go, browsing at my back. At sunset we get up and start down the other side of the mountains.

Down.

Gorge after gorge, turning, turning. Caverns of sunset, falling, falling away—just a single vast gold air breathed out by beings—they must have been marvelous beings, those gold-breathers. Down. Purple-and-green islands. Cleft and groined and gigantically pocked like something left behind after all the oceans vanished one huge night: the mountains. Their hills fold and fold again, fold away, down. Folded into the dens and rocks of the hills are ghost towns. Broken streets end in them, like a sound, nowhere. Shadow is inside. We walk (oh quietly) even so—breaking lines of force, someone's. Houses stand in their stones. Each house an empty socket. Some streaked with red inside. Words once went on in there—no. I don't believe that. Words never went on in there.

Down.

We circle, circle, circle again. Around each bend of the road, another, bending back. It is sunset. Look down: at the foot of the mountain something comes into view. Clustered on the water like wings, something shining. Something marveling at the float of its wings around it on the water—how they change and turn gold! That is what an evening was in the beginning, you once told me. *Y la paloma volvió a él a la hora de la tarde*. The photograph has been taken with the light behind it so that the two figures stand out clear against the mountains, which crush them from behind. They appear to be running—not because of the wolves who, as you see, are merely watching from this peak or that in mild curiosity. An effect of immediacy has been achieved by showing the figures close up and cut off at the knees. And the dove came into him in the evening.

Pilgrims were people to whom things happened that happen only once.

Trabadello   *17th of July*

> great moor
> answering heart
> oh do not forget
> the bounds of life keep shifting
>
> *Socho*

All day we steer along the edge of the mountains, looking up: the massif of Galicia. Tomorrow, climb again. "We will strike them in the name of God and of Saint James!" He is blithe. I am not. With folded paws they watch us, wait.

Cebreiro   *18th of July*

> in the town of Kowata
> there were horses to hire
> but I loved you so much
> I walked barefoot all the way
>
>   *Kan-ami*

So we climb to the top of the world once more. Straight up a rocky goat track, teetering, panting, pouring with sweat, plastered in dust to the pass of Cebreiro. At the top the wind is suddenly wide open and cold as a river. Look back—now it all pulls away at our feet, a thousand miles straight down straight back to the morning we began, it was a good bright morning in the eleventh century and we must have been very young, to judge from the photograph. So white was I when I went to harvest.

"I do not wish to sound Sokratic"—between angry bites of tortilla—"but what is your definition of penance?" He is annoyed with me today. He does not find my definition adequate. Pilgrims who go on foot but sleep in hotels (like us) are, in his view, more authentic than pilgrims who drive cars but sleep on the ground. Well, Galicia is a surprising place, is my view. And authenticity is surprisingly well defended here. For example, in this hotel, one huge white wolf guards us through the night. He has a huge, slow gaze and lies in the lettuces, still as a sculpture except for his black eyes which rove tirelessly back and forth over the moon-washed grounds. Who would have thought we would reach the zone of greatest danger to find that the wolves are the Hospitallers here? Penance can be a surprising study and pilgrims, even very authentic ones, raven in ways they do not expect. I have seen men die of the waters because they had learned to crave only wormwood. What sense could there be in that? What sense is there in pain at all—however we contrive it for ourselves as we cast about for ways to bind up the wound between us and God? The penitent in the act of binding up pain with pain is a photograph I have tried (unsuccessfully) a number of times to capture.

On the edge of the world is a black row of trees, shaking. Moon like a piece of skin above.

When is a pilgrim like a photograph? When the blend of acids and sentiment is just right.

To Samos

> *ah, for her too, it is the midnight pilgrimage*
> *how many of them there are! is this*
> *the work of hell?*
>
> *Chikamatsu*

What is the relation of rage to penance? Of entanglement?

It is a room of women. The night is black. In the photograph you can see an eyelid outlined in light from the street, here. The wall streaked with darker moisture, there. We listen to one another breathe. A cicada has got in here tonight and with his tiny rasp is nicking our nerve ends open. Even among the living, sometimes it seems a night will never end. A woman begins now to shriek, softly. I am not one to interfere, but sadness is sadness. Maybe a little song—my mother used to sing to me, sometimes at night, old ballads from the civil war:

> *as each hour passes, Miguel my love,*
> *you grow more dear:*
> *is that the reason, Miguel my love,*
> *you are not here?*

Ah. The shrieking has stopped. The others are breathing. The room grows quiet. Sometimes it is enough just to recognize a *camino*. Your bitter heart heals my heart, oh stay with me.

Samos   *19th of July*

> *"Yes," he says, "for your sake."*
> *What is he saying?*
>
>   *Zeami*

Penance is something broken off and thrown back, like a
sweetness that pierces your thoughts when all at once you
remember someone you dreamed of last night. It was someone
unknown. Just at dawn he was there, gleaming, shuffling. It
makes the night transparent to think of. It makes the night
incomparable. You dreamed of black arms shaking on the
edge of the world. Reaching back for that, you drop through
a freedom so clear it is simply pain. *Corazón nuevo* means
"new heart." It is a place you reach for through your skin,
which goes silver, through shame burned black on you,
through a thirst that we cannot describe, to where he is cooling
his wings in the stars like a pond, looking down at them trail-
ing around him on the dark water—look, there he is, vaguely
marveling—oh beloved, who could catch your eye?

Palas del Rey   *21st of July*

> *two petals fall*
> *and the shape of the peony*
> *is wholly changed*

>   *Shikibu*

Climbing and tracking through the bottomlands of Galicia in
deep fog. Shapes of life loom and vanish at us, grow grotesque.
Fog invents the imagination. We do not like to be surrounded
by meaningless grotesquerie, we are animals who take it upon
ourselves to find form in the misshapen. There (photographs)
is Velazquez on a cabbage stalk, and the pine trees here a row
of teeth? A fortress? Dice? And this fence post has the outline
of the Dead Sea, I believe.

Shapes of life change as we look at them, change us for
looking. Take wolves. You may think you know what a wolf
looks like: Queen Lupa thought so. For the countryside
around Palas del Rey was once thick with wolves and Lupa
was their queen, commanding them from a rough fort called
the Castro Lupario. Strange her yellow eyes should fasten one
day on Saint James himself.

He had come through Galicia in the first century A.D. on
his way to Finisterre, bent on Christianizing the uttermost
edge of the known world, and returned some years later to
Palestine to be martyred. Whereupon his disciples took the
body and embarked on a boat. They reached Galicia, within

sight of the Castro Lupario: see Lupa's eyes narrow. She goes to meet them and offers them land to bury the saint. Her speech is fluent, her face empty as a pocket and her plan is to kill them with death. That very night she sends the holy men out with the body on a cart. What are those animals yoked to the cart? Oxen, says Lupa. They look somehow darker, but at night who can say? Of course they are Lupa's own wolves—is this just a name? As they walk through the dark the wolves become oxen and pull the car to a good high hill. There the apostles build their tomb and offer thanks. Lupa's eyes widen. She studies the photographs under various magnifying lenses and, in the end, converts to the new religion.

Animals who ride on top of one another become entangled in ways they do not expect. From behind its back you may see a wolf as a queen, or a hill as a holy body or action as a fact. But facts form themselves this way and that, when we look for them in photographs or historical accounts.

Penance is one form we find, one form we insist on.

To Compostela   *23rd of July*

> *it's not easy to tell which end*
> *is which of a resting snail*
>
> Kyorai

Your voice I know. It had me terrified. When I hear it in dreams, from time to time all my life, it sounds like a taunt—but dreams distort sound, for they send it over many waters. During these hard days, I, a pilgrim, am giving my consideration to this. I trudge along the bottom of the river and the questioning goes on in me. What are we made of but hunger and rage? His heels rise and fall in front of me. How surprised I am to be entangled in the knowledge of some other animal. I know the animal. Does that mean I hand myself over? What is knowing? That is the question no one was asking, although I went from place to place and watched and listened to all that they said. I began to suspect some code was in operation. It had me terrified. Why? It plunged me in a pit, why? Because it is your question.

Your question I leave to you. There is in it a life of love I can scarcely look at, except in dreams. Or from time to time in photographs. Here is an old picture of My Cid with his mother. He is reaching up to put his hat on her head. Even before her illness she disliked being exposed to the afternoon sun. Yet she never brought a hat, and I believe they walked most afternoons. "Must get a hat," she would say every time, bending her head. Half smile.

How is a pilgrim like a blacksmith? He bends iron. Love bends him.

To Compostela   *24th of July*

> *why, my dear pilgrim hat*
> *you must accompany me*
> *to view the plum trees!*
>
> Basho

It takes a long time to arrive from not very far away. Just before the end we climb the small hill called Monte del Gozo. On achieving this height, from which the long-desired city can suddenly be seen half a league distant, ancient pilgrims would fall to their knees, shed tears of joy and begin to sing the Te Deum. "They felt like seafarers on reaching a haven after a tempest at sea," says one old account, which My Cid is reading aloud as he walks ahead of me. His voice is joy, his steps are joy, moved along like a waterwheel in water. While for my part I feel I have broken in half. Every pilgrim hits the mark in his own way.

Stars are spitting out of the cathedral as we enter Compostela: the cathedral! No it is not a mirage, this stupendous humming hulk of gold that stands as if run aground upon the plaza at the center of the city of Santiago. Built in the early years of the twelfth century, it was embellished toward the end of that century by one Master Mateo, who added the Portal of Glory to replace the original entrance. That was an act of grace. An entrance is important to a pilgrim: there can be only one.

An entrance should be a door built as a kiss, so Master Mateo understood it. All over his Portal are creatures in glory, harping with the harps of God. Smiles and half smiles fall from them like music. Animals and prophets, angels and the unnamed people of God raise their hands (surprised) and lean together in joy. Some show a small blush on each cheek. Through this portal, since the twelfth century, pilgrims enter. Won and not cheaply! They go straight in. They go to greet the Master of the place, entering with hand outstretched—I did it too (photograph). You approach the tree of Jesse, carved on the main column shaft by Master Mateo in 1195. You fit your hand into the five hollows visible at shoulder height among the tendrils of the tree. With your fingers in the hollows you can just lean down and kiss the head of Master Mateo, who has sculpted himself into the column base amid entangled leaves and animals. So many pilgrims' lips have brushed the hard plane of the Master's forehead that it has been worn into a convex pool, where rainwater and other moistures collect. *Se abandona.* (I like this photograph of two hurried visitors mistaking Master Mateo for a font.)

Stars, as I say, are shooting from the cathedral high into the air as we make our way across the plaza. They drop to the ground and lie in white fire. My Cid is bending down, in the photograph, to see whether he has one lodged in the sole of his sandal: in fact he does—problematic, you would think. But this is an example of the way trials turn to joy for him. Since an accident in childhood his legs have been of unequal length, but now, with a star in his shoe he is walking evenly for the first time in years. It has tripled his insouciance. He embraces a statue of Saint James. He embraces me—and I fall over (I have had several glasses today)—my good black beret rolling in the dust. "Why, I'm drunk!" "Why, I know." Half smile. With a certain flourish he replaces my beret.

Compostela   *25th of July*

> since you are blind
> your sense of poetry
> can't be expected to show on your face
>
>   Zeami

At midnight, fireworks in the plaza. No photographs—you know what fireworks are like. Tawdry, staggering, irresistible, like human love. Live stars fall on twenty thousand people massed in a darkened square. Some cry out, get burned, applaud. No star falls on me, although I try to position myself. Will you say you cannot make out my face in the dark? you heartless creature.

At the end of the fireworks we burn down the cathedral, as is traditional. So dazed with light and sulfur by now, there is no question it is the appropriate finale. Tomorrow morning, when we try to celebrate Saint James's solemn Mass amid the charred ruins, we will think again. But fireworks are always now, aren't they? like human love. *¡Corazón arriba!*

When is a pilgrim like the middle of the night? When he burns.

Compostela   *25th of July*

> even I who have no lover
> I love this time
> of new kimonos

> *Ontsura*

Notwithstanding a rainy morning in Compostela, solemn Mass in honor of Saint James is a debonair event. Pilgrims stand knee-deep in gold rubble, beneath swaying shreds of the high lantern, from which fire is still dropping in lit flakes. Soot and rain stream down on their shoulders unnoticed. The chancel is rumored to be a molten lake and small animals drowning in the side aisles, but we cannot see past a barrier of klieg lights and recording apparatus that has been set up in the central vault by National Spanish Television (the festival Mass will be broadcast live, with excerpts for the six o'clock news). Camera crews, trying to string booms across the nave, dodge and curse as they wade on the glassy sea.

There are several fine moments—for example, just about midway thorough the Credo, the central chandelier begins to shortcircuit, exploding a drizzle of stars over pilgrims in the front pews, quite spectacular. All applaud. But I see you peering hard at another photograph. Oh yes.

That solid-silver asteroid is the *botafumeiro,* a vessel from which incense is dispensed at the close of the festival Mass, to sanctify the crowds. It hangs straight down from the lantern of the church on a silver rope, about the size of a full-grown wolf. Beneath it, as you see, crowds of pilgrims are packed tight as fish all down the central aisle of the church, while the transepts are empty—why? It is to create a sort of runway: when the crowds are blessed, the *botafumeiro* is swung the whole width of the church—sixty-five meters from transept to transept—in great fuming swerves that carry our prayer up to God and drown the stench of new hearts as they burn below. Saint James tilts his brim: sixty-five meters across! Never was My Cid so happy.

Tomorrow, the ultimate absurdity. We will hire a car and drive to Finisterre.

Compostela   *26th of July*

> *the eye you see isn't*
> *an eye because you see it*
> *it's an eye because it sees you*
>
> Machado

Just as no mountain ends at the top, so no pilgrim stops in Santiago. The city and the saint buried there are a point of thought, but the road goes on. It goes west: Finisterre. So, although a pilgrim arrives in Compostela thinking he wants nothing more than to stop, and although the city entangles his feet so that for a day or two days or a week he stands still, or walks from statue to statue kissing Saint James, or lies on a bed in a dream, comes a day he awakens. Morning is cutting open its blue eyes. Time is a road. Time to go: Finisterre.

It would not be amiss to mention here one or two things about this place. The farthest western point of the landmass of Europe, a point sought by earliest Celtic inhabitants of the continent and made the object of pilgrimages centuries before Saint James was born, it is located on a spit of the Atlantic coast of Spain called Cabo de Finisterre. You can walk there. You can walk no farther (west).

Why did pilgrims and others searching to pinpoint the end of the world go always toward the west? For gold, says My Cid. As you travel west, days are longer: gold, more gold, and still more gold. However that may be, it is an endeavor as old as civilization to set out on a road that is supposed to take you to the very end of things, if you keep going. What do you find there? That is a good question. Who would you be if you knew the answer? There is one way to find out. So a pilgrim sets off. One thing is certain, one item is constant in the set of beliefs with which he travels. It is simply this, that when you reach the place called the end of the world, you fall off into the water. Some pilgrims drown, some do not. *Claro.*

How is a pilgrim like a No play? His end is not the point. And yet it is indispensable, to the honor and to the shame.

To Finisterre   *26th of July*

> *if we pick them*
> *we'll pick by guessing*
> *white chrysanthemums*
> *when first frost has settled*
> *and deceives the eye*
>
> *Mitsune*

In all honesty I am, when the time comes, unenthusiastic about proceeding to Finisterre. I slept heavily through the night and dreamed I was a criminal on the run from the local authorities. When they corner me in a cellar I hurl at them marrow bones, which explode in the air like live stars. Now dark and unshaven I crouch over my breakfast and *jump* when My Cid comes up behind my back. Conversation is balky. He taps a glass with a spoon. I page through the guidebook and find no entry for Finisterre. Is it a place of any interest? He grasps his beard. "Perhaps not." Half smile. "There is nothing there except the end of the world." And so we go to Finisterre.

There is only one road out of Compostela and we take it. Fog closes over us as we drive west. Hours pass. Blurring. Whitening. Fog keeps folding in. Outside—there is no outside. No presence at all out there. Abruptly the road ends. We stop. Disembark. Lock the car. Start to walk. A path is visible now and again through rents in the fog. We make our way along it for some time. Suddenly the path vanishes. There is not a cry. Not a living thing. Just white. Boulders come forward. We begin to climb over them, down, slipping, clutching at roots and lichen. Until the rocks go no farther. We grope this way. That way. There is nowhere to go. Still, we are not at the end. Eyes sting with peering. Cold air from some ice age is pulsing up out of the raw lungs under the sea. Foghorns go around, go off. Distances pass each other, far out. And a cry of some animal—white. Cold. "Shall we go back?" We begin to retreat the way we came, hand over hand, up the rocks. Fog is still shifting in, white, burning. Nothing is visible. And by now we are utterly lost. Let me revise that. I am lost. Suddenly pressingly alert I look around. No one is here but me. And there is no road.

How is a pilgrim like an epigram? Ask me tomorrow.

Finisterre

> *a dried salmon*
> *a pilgrim's gauntness*
> *both in the coldest season*
>
> Basho

There is a fearful ashy light falls on the end of the world. It makes the photographs slow. But you can see the scorched place and the immense hour. Eyes search the shore. There is no wind. There is no shadow. One flat event moves out in a ripple over the whole expanse of the water toward the line of the horizon. Still as watchers they stand, they look, moving their lips. They begin to approach. Now they are browsing at my back, where I have fallen at the edge of the water, knocking back and forth slightly in the force of the waves. They are leaning over me. What is it they are saying? Perhaps—no. Words never went on in me.

But one of them is bending closer. Fear shakes me. As it sometimes will just when we are about to be handed over. Your action is simple. You take hold of my paws and cross them on my breast: as a sign that I am one who has been to the holy city and tasted its waters, its kinds.

Pilgrims were people who carried little. They carried it balanced on their heart.

¡E ultreja e sus eja Deus adiuva nos!

Very Narrow:
Introduction to Just for the Thrill

> *Water is best.*
>
> Pindar

> *Memory is of the past.*
>
> Aristotle

> *No that's not her.*
>
> my father

Surely the world is full of simple truths that can be obtained by asking clear questions and noting the answers. "Who is that woman?" I overheard my father ask my mother one night when I was coming down the stairs to the kitchen. It took me a moment to realize he was asking about me—not because I did not know by then that he was losing his mind, which was obvious in other ways, but because he used the word *woman*.

I was not "woman" to him. I stopped halfway down the stairs. It reminded me of a night when I was twelve or thirteen. Coming down the same stairs, I heard him in the kitchen talking to my mother. "Oh, she won't be like them," he was saying with a sort of glow in his voice. It was the last time I heard that glow. Because soon afterward I did, to my dismay, begin to be like them—as the Chinese proverb says, "There was blood in the water trough early one morning."

I am not a person who feels easy talking about blood or desire. I rarely used the word *woman* myself. But such things are the natural facts of what we are, I suppose we have to follow out these signs in the endless struggle against forgetting. The truth is, I lived out my adolescence mainly in default of my father's favor. But I perceived that I could trouble him less if I had no gender. Anger tired him so. I made my body as hard and flat as the armor of Athena. No secrets under my skin, no telltale drops on the threshold. And eventually I found —a discovery due, in fact, to the austerities of pilgrimage— that I could suppress the natural facts of "woman" altogether. I did so. Unfortunately by then his mind was too far gone to care.

I lived alone for a long time.

What happened to me after that takes the form of a love story, not so different from other love stories, except better documented. Love is, as you know, a harrowing event. I believed in taking an anthropological approach to that.

Even now it is hard to admit how love knocked me over. I had lived a life protected from all surprise, now suddenly I was a wheel running downhill, a light thrown against a wall, paper blown flat in the ditch. I was outside my own language and customs. Why, the first time he came to my house he walked straight into the back room and came out and said, "You have a very narrow bed." Just like that! I had to laugh. I hardly knew him. I wanted to say, Where I come from, people don't talk about beds, except children's or sickbeds. But I didn't. Humans in love are terrible. You see them come hungering at one another like prehistoric wolves, you see something struggling for life in between them like a root or a soul and it flares for a moment, then they smash it. The difference between them smashes the bones out. So delicate the bones. "Yes, it is very narrow," I said. And just at that moment, I felt something running down the inside of my leg. I had not bled for thirteen years.

Love is a story that tells itself—fortunately. I don't like romance and have no talent for lyrical outpourings—yet I found myself during the days of my love affair filling many notebooks with data. There was something I had to explain to myself. I traveled into it like a foreign country, noted its behaviors, transcribed its idioms, prowled like an anthropologist for the rare and unwary use of a kinship term. But kinship itself jumped like a frog leg, then lay silent. I found the kinship between a man and a woman can be a steep, whole, excellent thing and full of languages. Yet it may have no speech. Does that make sense?

One night—it was the first winter my father began to have trouble with his mind—I was sitting at the kitchen table wrapping Christmas presents. I saw him coming down the stairs very slowly, holding his hands in front of him. In his hands were language and speech, decoupled, and when he started to talk, they dropped and ran all over the floor like a bag of bell clappers. "What happened to you to I who to? There was a deer. That's not what I. How many were? No. How? What did you do with the things you dripped no not dripped how? You had an account and one flew off. That's not. No? I. No. How? How?" He sat down all of a sudden on the bottom step and turned his eyes on me, clearly having no idea in the world who I was, or how he came to be there with me, or what should happen next. I never saw a human being so naked. His face the face of a fledgling bird, in what fringe of infant evening leaves, in what untouched terror lapped.

Sometimes you come to an edge that just breaks off.

The man who named my narrow bed was a quiet person, but he had good questions. "I suppose you do love me, in your way," I said to him one night close to dawn when we lay on the narrow bed. "And how else should I love you—in your way?" he asked. I am still thinking about that.

Man is this and woman is that, men do this and women do different things, woman wants one thing and man wants something else and nobody down the centuries appears to understand how this should work. "Every day he'd come in from the fields and throw his old filthy hat on my clean tablecloth that we're going to eat off—sweatband down!" says my mother, still furious, and he's been gone how long? years now.

Just for the Thrill:
An Essay on the Difference Between
Women and Men

China City, Indiana

Rattling through the ghost cornfields of Indiana at 3:00 a.m. under a gold slipper moon, with handfuls of fog throwing themselves at the windshield and Ray Charles on the radio, I am thinking the difference between women and men is a boundless sea. *You can reach the opposite shore if you repent,* says classical Chinese wisdom. *You turned my night into day you made my dreams come true,* says Ray Charles, *you thrill you.* We have been driving since early morning, since the bold, serious green hills of Virginia, since a mountain pass where General Jackson was shot by his own men on an ink black night in 1863. Cross fire. After cross fire there is not much to talk about. What is love like for you? is a question I am not finding a way to ask as the dark thrill miles go ghosting by and old Earth begins turning toward her meteor showers of midsummer. Watching the edge of his face in the dark, something comes at me. You. Thrill. You.

Indiana, Route 40

I was thinking about concubinage last night as we drove across West Virginia in a thunderstorm. Hour after hour crossing down, mountain after mountain down and around, down through mining towns that flashed steep and white in sudden lightning like the plan of one endless accident. Sometimes as many as three hundred girls at once from the general population around Peking were admitted to the Forbidden City, he was explaining to me. Aged nine to fourteen. Who became the emperor's property. Who were likened to jade yet said to remain fragrant. The back of the truck is full of dictionaries and language tapes. He is an anthropologist of China, using this trip across America to study up on classical Chinese. A language consisting, so far as I can judge, entirely of wisdom. For example, *In love women get what they want, men what they need.* Well it was about a year ago, we became lovers, all I wanted was for the pulling to stop. Pulling pulling pulling. It was pulling on my arms. Pulling on my eyes. Pulling on my lungs. Pulling on the sweat on the backs of my legs. Pulling at night, pulling all day, pulling not falling, not burning, not matter, what does pulling matter? "It's only love," he would say, laughing, opening my clothes. He called our flesh "this luxury." "No luxury is endless," I said, and he said, "That's okay, we don't have much time." Love made him so happy I began calling him the emperor of China. There were places where luxury dropped away, where I waited. I saw something flash open then lost it.

Lachine, Quebec

It was about a year ago he appeared at the door of my office. A thunder-sullen autumn afternoon, I had all the lights on. Had spoken to him once before at a party, I think. He came in. Smiled. Sat down. Began talking about Chinese art. Behind him the door stood open, the corridor slowly emptied, darkness came in. I was thinking, Well it will take some getting used to that scratchy voice of his. Finally I said I had to go home. He stood up. Smiled. Went out. Two days later he was there again. Closed the door behind him. Walked around the desk. Smiled. That scratchy voice. "I just came in here to kiss on you," he said. I had to laugh, what makes a woman laugh? "Kiss on you," this odd expression. It came at me like a light particle from outer space. A year later I laughed again, when he said we should take the truck and drive across America, camping in forest preserves, all the way to Los Angeles. Well language lives in alteration, here I am. Take two-measure words and press them together like lips of a wound. *Emperor, concubine, fire, paper.* Love too much, love at all.

Oriole, Indiana

Listening to ancient trees stream upward in the China black rain night of Indiana and the long river sound goes plundering, harpooning past. Lying on my back with arms folded on the chest, a posture I find helpful for thinking, while beside me the emperor sleeps. Forest birds perch together all night but when day breaks, who the enemy is is no longer clear. Drops of water from a leak in the roof of the tent are hitting my forehead one after another like items on a list. I am bad at building a fire. Bad at folding the tent. Bad at driving the truck. Bad at sticks. Bad at snakes. Bad at coffee. Bad at

clothesline. Bad at knives. Bad at water fetching. Bad at un-
packing. Bad at packing. Bad at shortwave radio tuning. Well
the anthropology of camping is a hardy subject. We can trace
it back at least as far as the summer of 1553, when the Hades
emperor of China packed up the imperial court, including
three hundred palace women and the household goods loaded
on 1,110 carrying trays, and trekked them to the Ta'o River
region to view the landscape. His consort at the time was the
forty-year-old Lady Cheng, with whom he shared delight in
the printed page—nearly one hundred trays of poetry, essays,
medical textbooks, drama, detective novels and pornography.
From the emperor's own brush we have four sheets of calligra-
phy on what made a woman a woman, what made her part her
lips and close her eyes. It is a beautiful scroll, in the dry and
lean style cultivated by that period.

Dawn. The emperor turns in his sleeping bag. Opens his
eyes. Smiles and says quietly, "Fuck me." *Bad at pelting the rat
for fear of smashing jade bowl beside it,* says classical Chinese
wisdom. Lady Cheng's special interest was mapmaking.

Lachine, Quebec

To desire and be desired, what could be simpler? A woman
cannot tell a simple story, my father used to say. Well here is
what it looks like on the videotape. You see desire go travel-
ing into the total dark country of another soul, to a place
where the cliff just breaks off. Cold light like moonlight falling
on it.

It was a full-moon night about a year ago, the first time I went to his house. I wore a gray dress with buttons, and not telling him that it was the first night I went to any man's house, ate chicken. Then he so carefully washed each pot. Standing at the sink he rinsed each pot. Standing there he dried each pot. And said. Turning, "I like this dress." (Why?) "Because there are so many ways to take it off."

Who thinks herself a treasure is soon parted from it, says classical Chinese wisdom. What makes life life and not a simple story? Jagged bits moving never still, all along the wall.

Alton, Indiana

It is easy to get lost in Indiana, all the cornfields look alike and I am no help with the map. At 4:00 a.m., too tired to think about the tent, we fall out of the truck and sleep on the grass of the Holly Mount Holiness Church. Now it is dawn, hot silver fog solid over the cornfields. The emperor lies wrapped in sleep. I beat it down to the river where the dark Ohio Nile is filling its reed banks under a slowly heating sky. River life meditates on its surface. The still boats. Black green silver. Fishermen caught in tiny attitudes. Silver green black. I am thinking about arranged marriages, their economy. First you marry, then you come to know, then you fall in love with. Those three things. Marriage does not interest the emperor but economy does. "A tent has two uses," he said glancing at the sky one rainless night.

It was a Tuesday in October when the Hades emperor,

then fourteen years old, was married for political reasons to the daughter of a commoner hastily given an army commission. The day after the wedding the emperor chose nine new concubines at his mother's direction and was making merry with them late into the night. Academicians record that one of the women, instructed by the emperor to sing obscene or unfamiliar songs, refused and was sentenced to death on the spot—a penalty carried out symbolically by clipping the tassel of her hair. (The attendant who tried to intervene was served sixty strokes with the whipping club. He survived but, it was noted, lost one buttock.) Lady Cheng kept the clippings until the emperor's burial in 1601.

Anthropology, like marriage, is an activity of the forebrain. If we strain thought clear of impulse slowly, slowly the day scream subsides to ordered lust. *Living dog better than dead lion,* says classical Chinese wisdom. If you are going down it is a wall. That is my message. Climb the wall.

Celine Lake, Indiana

Camping is hard on top vertebrae. Baked Indiana clay is no silk pillow. It reminds me of the morning my father woke up so angry, he dislocated his neck getting out of bed. On the good side, he loved mileages and every Sunday took us out in the car to view the landscape. As we rolled down the driveway he would glance at the odometer and call out, *"Now somebody remember this number!"* I was somebody. I remembered that number. For hours, for years.

It is my belief that women like to be given a task in the middle. Don't worry about putting up the tent, just hold this pole. Just fill this pail. Just chop this onion. Just collect sticks all this size. Timing is important in the middle, I know when the cursing stops is the time I go hold up the pole. Exactitude is important, depending on what the numbers are for, but I usually don't find that out until after. Good temper is important, caryatids often outlive the structures into which they are built. And now—tent pegs scorching my hands, I can hear his voice saying, *For God's sake don't grow up to be one of those helpless women.* Father was a man who knew the right way to do things. Well it's true the natural facts generally elude me. Yet, to see it catch like a row of wheat and do nothing, just stand there, face growing hot, knuckles hanging down— collaborator! That is who I am. Women are not pure and they know it is the reason why the middle smells so good. *A person without a smiling face should not open a shop,* says classical Chinese wisdom. The original Chinese ideogram for *woman* shows her in a bowing position. Later the character was reduced to that of someone kneeling. For ease in writing.

Indian Lake, Indiana

Camping is union with the Tao. *Drop your form and body, reject your hearing and eyesight, forget your place in the hierarchy of things, then you may become one with the infinite,* classical Chinese wisdom counsels. In Indiana we are camped inside a solid black Tao of crickets. Night is a house, this one sound its walls. Ear stops at listening, mind stops at matching, spirit forgets the ten thousand things. We lie side by side in the dark, two halves of a knucklebone—the same knucklebone? Crickets are.

Illinois, Route 19

Cornfield after cornfield after cornfield. Through southern Illinois and across sullen Missouri where the ends of the sky fall open and into hot Kansas where they dropped and stay. *Another thing is you know one thing is,* Carmen Macrae is singing on the radio, *I don't want to be free.* One thing camping is is an excellent way to confront the difference between women and men. The emperor is videotaping out the window while I drive. Explaining to me that in classical Chinese the character for *cornfield* plus the character for *oneself* mean freedom. Well I came on this trek to leave one self behind. Like a painting, it will be erased, I thought, and the suffering too. For desire is like the secret of the suffering of a work of art, dispersed over the surface of the beloved's body, residing everywhere and nowhere at once. *You know I'd rather be a blind girl.* I came on this trek to videotape desire—to obtain cheap, prompt and correct facts about an object to which nothing in the world exactly corresponds. *Than to see you walk away with another love.*

Marthasville, Missouri

What is it men want? They talk of pleasure. They go wild, then limp, then fall asleep. Is there something I'm not getting? Classical Chinese wisdom recognizes five conditions of getting. It is not like. It is like. It is just like. It is only like this and not like anything else. It is. The ultimate nature of conditions, for example, is just like water. The ultimate nature of water is like the pleasure of men. The ultimate nature of the pleasure of men is not like the pleasure of women. A Missouri thunderstorm racing across the sorghum fields with its huge dragon paws dropping the sky open, you can stand and watch it come toward you for half a day and not know if it is near or far off, you can see it fold back into itself and vanish conditionless as water—is not like anything else, is only like this. The air is dark as murder. Radio crackles. *Standin' in the rain*, Robert Johnson is singing. *Ain't a drop fell on me*. Is it true men envy women their way of making love? Slow and spiritual is how the emperor describes it. *My clothes is all wet*. Sometimes he closes his eyes and says, "Make me your boy slut." *But my flesh is dry as can be*.

Kansas, Route 6

Light lopes along the wall. We are driving west, there is the limitless green limit of the horizon. Clouds bigger than clouds. I am wondering about the color green. Why it hurts like sound hurts inside a jar. I can see it speeding up every stalk two hundred miles away. But the emperor is in an historical mood today. He knows a lot about the American experience. In the 1880s when settlers first came to the 80th parallel in Kansas, they knew it would be dry but, believing prayer could influence climate, which for about ten years or so sure enough it did, they named the towns names like Burma and Memphis and laughed at the light. Then the wind changed. And the immortal diamond forepang struck them like matches, burned them to the ground. This is not what he is saying but it is what I know. I am the one who watches the way plants sweat at noon come at me, slap my mind across the room. That is who I am, those three things.

Kansas City, Kansas

In camping, cryptic rituals of the lost tribe confront the anthropologist. I am learning to read a map. There are many small numbers. I navigate us across Kansas and into a large ruined area where crumpled fenders and auto parts are lying about. It is hard to find the exit. "Women don't know maps, I never met a woman who could read a map," says the emperor. Well I haven't been a woman for long, I will keep working on maps. They imitate reality in somewhat the same way sex does desire, curtly. *Make me your fuck boy,* I hear one of us whispering in the midst of dark tent nights—where do I go for a map into that country?

Lawrence, Kansas

Camping is a system of mutually enacted paradoxes, like any lost tribe—outside and inside, space and surface, love and lust. Be careful they reverse. Nonetheless I am learning to build a fire. It has a lot to do with lining up sticks in regimented sizes. I enjoy ranking my sticks. By the time I finish, it is too late for breakfast, we drive to town for lunch. "Paper is fire; fire is paper," says the emperor, citing classical Chinese wisdom. I am not sure this helps me but I will keep working. Enlightenment is not a place, no use rushing to get there.

Lawrence, Kansas

Concubinage is what linguistic anthropologists call a "limit accusative in the grammar of desire." *Bed* requires no preposition, a simple verb of motion. Simple. Simple nights. Whir. Click. True. I keep trying to tell the truth, kept trying, to you, to him, in the words that were there. "The camera gives cheap, prompt and correct facts to the public," said Nam June Paik in his 1957 video essay, *No Idea of the Holy*. But my facts slip through the language like a glimpse of the lost tribe.

It was a still night in October the first time I went to his house. The trees hung quiet. We stood by the bed. Tuesday. Part of my mind was listening to the quiet outside, part was staring appalled at him unfastening the buttons of my dress. Beginning from the top. One by one. Some men are as orderly as women, I was thinking. I wonder will I bleed? And I said,

"I feel so lonely," and he said, "Lie down and tell me about it."

You could videotape only feet for example. Only feet of women. Only feet of women wearing ankle bindings.

Lawrence, Kansas

Enlightenment is useless but some of its principles are not—for example, unconventionality. This means if you see someone struggling, help him don't ask what the object is. *A million maggots in a silk hat,* says classical Chinese wisdom. The emperor likes the idea of making love to women fitted with false penises. I try not to neglect anything that is part of him. It is rather like watching somebody die.

Lawrence, Kansas

Four days in Lawrence. Car trouble. The glue is getting thin. I am hard to wake in the morning. I pull hot blue Kansas over my head and lie still until the emperor goes off to work on the car. Sound of heating blue sky. Smell of grass scraping the light. Crickets a solid nerve wall. What is behind the veil? Fall asleep again. Into the long glass nightmare, a pilgrimage to a distant mountain. The others had already set off hours ago. Heartsick and filthy, I am rushing about the hotel trying to round up my gear. Drop my eyeglasses. On hands and knees desperately gathering the broken shards, then insert them into my eyeballs and rush out. The barren dome of the morning. The empty roadway. Its stones. Not even a stray dog.

I wanted to find one law to cover all of living, I found fear. A list of my nightmares is the map of the way out of here.

Kansas, Route 20

It is rock not water. Blue rule of the sky hammers heat down on us. I am talking with my eyes closed because the light hurts them. Today it is a light melted down and collected from the edges of razors. "Certainty is an illusion," the emperor is saying. "We live in a probabilistic world." *Not water. Rock.* Anthropologists cannot hear people who talk with their eyes closed, did you know that? "Anthropologists avoid such words as *perfect, correct, pure, total, final, ultimate, absolute,*" he continues, "such notions as true names. The Rockies, you know, were the Northern Andes in 1804, then the Shining Mountains, then the Enchanted Ones. Or take jazzmen. When jazzmen get to really jamming they call it eggplanting—did you know that?" *Rock.* What is love like for you? is a question that concerns also language. I am listening with my eyes closed so I can hear the wall. Every lost tribe protects certain words. This is the research that takes me late into the night, transcribing what I have learned while there is time—the forms, the harrow, the stranger in it. Something shattered inside the words we use. Love? If two lie together they have heat. Lover? Good lover. Better lover. Love being your lover. One of the best lovers I ever. Better than aubergine. Had. Had. Had. Stop the box.

Topeka, Kansas

Camping pulls your soul together as any martial art. Its Tao is manifest in, for example, knives. The emperor has a machete two feet long that sleeps beside him in the tent, a Swiss army knife, a spring blade, an Italian bread knife, an exactor, and four pairs of nail clippers. "Don't touch that," he said when I bent toward the machete one morning. "People tend to cut themselves on that." The spring blade came in handy the day we drove past a road-killed badger, its tail now swinging from the rearview mirror. *What kind of man are you?* Etta James is singing on the radio. *I just can't satisfy.*

On the day before Christmas my father and I used to go to the woods to cut a tree. Ploughing through deep snow in our high boots and big socks, the two trusty woodsmen. He carried the saw and the ax. "You'll cut yourself," he said. I followed him, shouting. "No. No. Yes," until we found the right tree. Stood while he cut. Watched while he trimmed. Together we dragged it home. But not last Christmas. *What kind of man are you?* Mother and I went about our tasks as usual—does burning matter? *No matter how I try.* He was upstairs in his pajamas and fedora, with old calendars spread out all around him, figuring out what day it was. It was Tuesday. I took the saw and the ax and went. It wasn't hard; I was happy chopping and the snow flying about. A fine balsam. I dragged it toward home. I was afraid. I knew he would be angry. I was watching the upstairs windows wondering, How angry? I came in through the back door, watching. He was there in the kitchen. He looked at the tree and the saw and the ax. It was something perfectly quiet. "I didn't think you could do that," he said. Perfectly quiet. His hands hanging down. The tiny ticking kitchen. The snow-dark morning. It was draining from him into me. I had killed him.

Verity, Kansas

A silo at night is a momentous place. Keen with old corn through the blackness. He stands exactly in the middle, making sounds that leave him to become whales of the sea booming and waking around the walls. Then the snuffed dark again. His cheekbones glisten, opium polish. Every line of his body is an iron hoop through me. Who can take on the diabolical in another human? Can you? Could you have comforted him?

Scott Lake, Kansas

Wind does not stop by day here, does not stop by night, it keeps belling, boasting, wrestling, rinsing, disheveling, bonfiring, boistering down—the black morning tea blows out of the cups. Even inside the tent I can hardly balance to pluck my eyebrows. Wind makes me sing. Think of all the women I am. The emperor however is powerfully one, a scholar of pleasure, ever on the vulture peak. Once in the midst of seducing a woman, he tells me, he scalded himself pouring water for tea. The result was to make love all night with left hand in a basin of ice.

Well enlightenment is useless, I said this often, no one

was listening. You may be an extraordinary master of classical wisdom yourself, no use making other people miserable. Try laying your rice paper directly on the campground to paint. The bumpy lines are like not knowing.

Colorado, Route 9

Here begin the sagebrush fields and true prairie land that never felt the plough. Clouds hunch down and tumble about on the horizon, then stop for afternoon. Flat miles of sky. The emperor is instructing me in the ten radicals that are the basis of the largest number of words in classical Chinese. These more important radicals, arranged in the order of their use, are. Water. Grass. Wood. Heart. Man. Hand. Silk. Wood. Advance or Go. Mouth. I am wondering why, if he wanted to make love, he paused for tea at all. The ten most prominent radicals appear in 1,090 words. Observe the interests suggested by them. The mere fact that the heart is the basis of one hundred words in a vocabulary of three thousand, he continues, indicates a high degree of moral interest. Ever far from the vulture's peak myself, I am wondering, What is the radical for "Frankie went down to the hock shop; she didn't go there for fun"? Watch the mountains. They stand clear. Remember that enlightenment is useless, that life is an action and its end is a mode of action not for tapping blood out of a thought. *Brush cannot write two words at the same time,* says classical Chinese wisdom. I watch the edge of his face, the bumpy lines.

Gunnison, Colorado

Camping is radical economy. We use the world for space, its light for fear. No liquor. Same foods. Few objects, but this is controversial. On my side of the front seat when we drive, on my side of the tent when we camp, I have three bottles for water, three notebooks with pens, three rosaries. The emperor is careful of them when we pack and unpack. He looks at them. He looks at me. We had a quarrel one night about half a year ago I remember, we traveled to that crude coast where everything breaks and turns simple again as a protein structure. According to Aristotle, there are three kinds of argument. The kind that shows and destroys. The kind that gets out emotion. The kind that makes big things small and small things big. The kind where a man says to a woman, "Well I guess you'll just have to watch me jack off a lot," Aristotle would call an effective use of standard names. After a quarrel, rooms are quiet. The hard little ash leaves were blowing against one another outside. Two small night rooms: in one a man is whistling, stops.

Colorado, Route 76

Take these chains from my heart. Going uphill to Colorado with Ray Charles on the radio we pass eleven thousand feet. *And set me free.* Go around a long rock corner and the motor stops dead. The emperor sits staring down at his hands on the steering wheel. Lays his forehead on his hands. Begins to curse steadily, quietly. But I am already gone, out of my side of the truck and over the boulders and down into the woods, gone. Make my way to the edge of the canyon and stand leaning hard against a day-warm rock. Whenever I say my rosary I feel wrong and right at the same time—do you know? watching shadows lengthen, sharpen, blacken down the mountainside. One thing I learned from my father is to stay out of sight while machinery is being fixed. Anger may come shrapneling at you. Who is this man? Are you getting some idea? Nowadays he is strapped to a chair in a room with three lunatics, but during the war my father was a navigator and flew low over France dropping parcels for spies—once, nylon stockings, hard to explain to the Germans who shot down the plane. *"Wo ist die Dame?"* they kept asking, but Father had no German and the other three were dead in their seats.

Colorado, Route 78

Driving is penance. Light like a slap across the bridge of the nose with a bat. I glance down. Hands on the steering wheel, tough skin pulling across the knuckles, are my father's hands. Gripping. Only once I saw his hands go slack. It was many years ago. Night, I came to the doorway like a sleep shape. He was sitting on the edge of the bed unable to rise. Facedown, one on each knee, were his hands, stunned. He sat there in the dark like a stopped train. In a night longer than a tunnel. In an ark suddenly open to all the winds.

Lake Isabel, Colorado

Dawn is cold. I inch out of the sleep nest, the emperor does not like to wake alone. But dawn is for prowling. No human language in the woods. I make my way along dark forest paths where wooden tables are set to catch the light, each foursquare with its own shadow. Each oddly gold like a story about to begin. Who set them in place? From the shadows run mysterious ground lines down into my apparent heart. Who is in me like a bell? Yes, enlightenment is useless but I am hurrying along with a lion in both legs, there is something here I want to explain. *If lions could talk we would not understand them,* says classical Chinese wisdom, but I know there is something here I can explain. I am rushing through the forest like a pile of roaring twigs and I am sure I can explain this if I get back in time. I arrive at camp breathless. Billie Holiday is on the radio, the smell of wood is hot, the emperor looks up. "Tables," I say. "Each shadow," I say. "The bell," I say. He is looking around him on the ground. "Could you get the coffee out of the truck?"

Well it's true I cannot tell a simple story. I lived alone for many years content with the reclusive life. *Nice work if you can get it.* But emperors do come along. He is measuring the coffee and telling me about Daruma dolls in classical China. "Daruma" was the slang nickname for courtesans, they were like the legless Buddha Daruma dolls that always spring back ready for more each time placed on their backs. *And you can get it if you try.*

Divide, Colorado

Altitudes race our strength to nothing. Camped now higher than the eight burning hells. Within a glass-timber morning we stumble about after the night of demons. It was 3:00 a.m. when the emperor leapt from his bedclothes shouting, *"Something is biting my nuts!"* A hornet I suggested. An angry father god he was sure. We scoured the blankets, he was weeping. I stood in the huge Colorado mountain darkness, training my flashlight on his parts. I have never been a warmhearted person. My father and I shook hands on Christmas, birthdays, and farewells. "Do you want to trade sleeping bags with me?" "Yes," he said very fast. We exchanged bedding. He lay rustling a long while and fell at last into mistrustful sleep. I viewed the stars. The summer constellations are complex. Far too many stars, late and young, shuddering. Many a classical master turns in old age more and more to brushwork to transmit the spirit beyond words.

Colorado, Route 38

The great basins of the sky are overturned here, clouds run loose. Air is too clear to be air, it punches objects out at you. To the west, mountains. And I believe that is the Arkansas River tumbling by, hilarious as a well-rested emperor. On the radio Ray Charles is singing, *Tell your mama tell your pa*. It seems to me the Arkansas River should be in Arkansas and the emperor explains why it is not. "Oh," I say. He glances at my face and begins the explanation again. Well it's true I have never been good at understanding explanations, my father pointed this out. Father spent long hours explaining, for example, the European banking system or how to tie a double-running bowline. Sweat running down my scalp, I listen very hard, I would listen very hard—so much depends on this for them—but in place of the explanation it fills up behind my eyes with a light like some terrible crystal. School was the same —panic and tactics and smiling hard. You can learn to seem rational. Once I saw a video of a roomful of deaf boys being taught to laugh, you just hold the sides of your ribs and shake rhythmically. *Tell your mama tell your pa.* But another time I saw an explanation of a different kind. *Goin' send you back to Arkansas.* A bleached blasted cold afternoon in March, I was looking out my window at birds dipping and diving in the bare branches of the ash trees in the courtyard, locking and unlocking. Not random play. There were four birds. While three sat watching, one flew out and positioned itself alongside a branch, then rose on its wings and dropped, describing in flight an imitation of the shape cut by the branch in air. They performed each in turn, then began again. They were without exhaustion or fear, as happy as proverbs placed into experience at just the point that turns a tale.

Monarch Pass, Colorado

Sheering down the other side of the Continental Divide we go level by level, lower and lower, into an emptied-out ocean of the world. Mountains gleam with light from before there was light. They are shaped like fingers but packed together for prayer. Where mountains cast shadows on other mountains is an eye-scalding place to be. Light instead of air here.

One who forgets about things and forgets about heaven is a self-forgetter, says classical Chinese wisdom. To forget the self is called entering heaven.

Telluride, Colorado

Peaks clamber onto peaks. Up over the shoulders of the mountains like eager tourists clouds come pressing. The emperor is cheerful after a night of luxuries. Although the love act with its various names does not interest me very much, I am by now a plausible anthropologist of his pleasure. "Make me your toy," he says. "Make me something special for yourself." I give thought to this while floating above the aspen trees. Hedonism comes naturally to men. At the sound of a key turning, a man has locks all over his body. But women are numb or liars or never stop thinking, you can not make me stop thinking. *Does a Flower Love to Have Its Ovary Sucked by a Bee?* is the title given by the Hades emperor of China to a treatise he composed during his camping trip of 1553. The scroll is very beautiful. So far as we know on the whole, a flower does not, he decided.

Ophir Needles, Colorado

The aspen trees are their own ocean. Dawn is clear, the emperor testy after a night of knee-clenching cold at eleven thousand feet in the Ophir Needles. We slept facing opposite directions. "They don't look like needles, do they look like needles to you?" I ask. But he is deep in study. He prefers to read at meals. Well I have work to do too. There are masters of classical Chinese wisdom who know the essential meaning of more than five thousand idioms, of which not a single one makes sense to me. Each is written with four characters. The strokes go horizontally from left to right and vertically from top to bottom. Here is one that means "Tortoise listens to monkey." Here is one that means "Fishermen listen to fox cries." Here is one that means "Courtesan listens to the rear end of her client." I will keep working on idioms.

It is interesting to note, something the emperor let fall in passing, that he has camped in the Needles before. Some years ago, he thinks it was with his first girlfriend but doesn't remember the details. Oh yes, he remembers she used to get little bruises on her hipbones from lovemaking. A light wind turns over the aspen leaves one by one.

Ophir Needles, Colorado

The word *exposure* means "panic"; in classical Chinese both are formed from the radical for *light*. We are camped entirely alone on a sun-drilled enormity of meadow like two pips in a spittoon. I crouch on the void. "What a beautiful place," says the emperor, rising and stretching against the sky. "Shall we go for a walk?" I shake my head. There is no use trying, I learned long ago in childhood, to explain why I prefer to remain under cover on wide-open days like this. He strides off through unfiltered space and sun and time to find a lake he heard about somewhere higher in the Needles. *That lucky old sun,* Ray Charles is singing on the radio. *Ain't got nothin to do.* I rest my hemorrhoids awhile then begin to wash brushes. *But roll around heaven all day.* To see your own true nature, even in the eye of a needle, is something. Once you saw it, you would become total and devise your own methods, childlike or not. I am studying the later brushwork of one of the most revered of the classical masters. There are big simple blocks and black tone bumps. To avoid weightiness he used ink that had been ground the day before and heavily sized paper that would not absorb it. The ink puddles force you toward him. *Just roll around heaven all day.* Well enlightenment is useless but the fact that the bridge does not quite reach the opposite shore adds a note of blissful mirth to his painting *Three Blind Men Crossing the Ta'o River.*

Ophir Needles, Colorado

Camping is an existence that possesses only relation. The emperor fails to return from his lake, I win a whole day to watch clouds pile past the mountain and contemplate the fact that I am an illusion. There is no self, the classical masters are firm on this. No Ahab. No Starbuck. No whale? It reminds me of the way my father would smile, the summer he began to lose his mind. He was falling away from himself in shreds, the inside became visible like bones hanging black and loose in the glare of an X ray. He would look down at himself and smile. Lips always moving. And I drew close, he was saying, "You bastard, you stupid bastard you goddamn stupid bastard you goddamn stupid useless bastard you."

Chill strands of twilight are hurrying in. I rise to greet the emperor and make illusory tea. Far overhead the stars burn. Not us. We are inflammable.

Ophir Needles, Colorado

Fumigating my hemorrhoids and viewing the tall characters of the aspen upside down begins another pure morning in camp. The emperor slept well, awoke sweet and is reading an American gangster novel in the shade. Young monk on the vulture peak. Vertical strokes of the aspen denounce evils—what evils? I am practicing to paint them. If black moss points are added to the aspen bark, it will begin to look like a very old tree, the technique is called "overburning." Used also in depicting courtesans. Earlier this morning I asked the emperor why Chinese paintings have writing on them. "Space is space," he said. "You can fill it with rocks or trees or words or heavy rain." "To cover the nakedness?" I asked. "To complete the design," he answered. Well, enlightenment is useless but if across the highest peaks one cloudless afternoon shadows are moving, I know how to brush like the old P'an master with inks ground for a different day.

Sugar City, Colorado

Love makes you an anthropologist of your own life. What are these ceremonies and why should we take part in them? What is this language we have got backed up into on long worst fire nights like a bad translation? It is important to keep recording the dialect forms, tracking the idioms. Yes there is a violence in it. *Ask the badger for its hide,* says classical Chinese wisdom. A dialect will sound like your own language to you, only despoiled somehow, hung up by the tail. Late at night I sit in the truck transcribing my notes by flashlight, tape quality is poor. There is a nucleus of terms I never get right. (Pleasure). "Pleasure? You know what pleasure is—fun." "Is pleasure important?" "Yes." "Is language important to pleasure?" "No." "When you say, Enjoy me, what does that mean?" "Means I want you to have pleasure too." "Who am I?" "You? My partner. We're such good partners," he mumbles by now falling asleep—*then why am I so utterly alone?* But the tape broke before this.

Dolores River, Colorado

Cold morning, loud rivers. River water jumping, sparkling, lavishing itself down the riverbed. Pine shadows hard on the ground. Tempers ragged in camp. Hearts that do not view one another, how different from hearts viewing not one another. I eat cucumbers in the shade while the emperor drugs himself and goes on with his study of classical Chinese idioms, alone in the empty hall. Broken ink is the name of a brush technique used sparingly by the classical masters. The brush starts out rich and black but gradually dries, until the bristles are moving separately and leaving areas of white exposed to view like sudden bones. Also called flying white in virtue of its effect, a very desirable effect of speed and freedom.

Montrose, Colorado

Camping is an exercise in mind's abstinence. When everything has disappeared into the light, *everything has disappeared* appears. It is the inversion of dreams replacing sleep. It is time to go to a motel. The emperor is surprisingly docile. "You choose," he says as we cruise the motel strip of Montrose. "These places all look like whorehouses to me." "Whorehouses," in his accent, takes me by surprise. I blush to the backs of my eyes. On the radio, Ray Charles is singing "Beautiful Maria of My Soul," a song that exists in twenty-two versions. *Love makes fools, fools make love.*

I awake blank at 4:00 a.m. The motel room has drained itself out the back like an eyeball. When I am unable to sleep, I lie quietly and make a list of differences between me and Kafka. Kafka had thirty-seven dreams in his life and only one concerned sexual activity. In the dream Kafka goes to a brothel with his friend Max. They each choose a girl. Amid sport Kafka has two thoughts. First he thinks, This is so much fun why isn't she asking me to pay? *Not the same fools.* Second, he observes that her back, when she turns away, is covered with big red circles that are coming off on his hands like wax when he touches her—as though from a crumbled seal. *Not the same love.* He awakes blank at 4:00 a.m.

Mesa Verde, Colorado

Camping is an immense life-form in which many small consciousnesses are working away like roots. Captive themselves. Taking on its color. Inching downward. At Mesa Verde we are camped chockablock with hostages from other places, Nevada, Japan, dogs, each on a gravel pad just big enough for the car, tent, clothesline and radio if you put the radio on top of the car. *I guess I just like to dream.* One tree each. It is prohibited to camp anywhere but on the gravel pad. It is forbidden to make fire except in the pit provided. It is unlawful to walk or move except on the trails marked. It is not permitted to appropriate, excavate or destroy any object of antiquity you may find. Billie Holiday is singing on the radio, *Of a cottage by a stream.* It is unacceptable to bite out parts of your face from inside and spit them at the blue nonstop volcano sky. *With my man.* The emperor is busy in the fire pit, cooking chicken with his headset on, dancing a little and repeating classical Chinese idioms. *A waterfront pavilion gets the moonlight first. Sure as eggs. Climb the wall.*

Mesa Verde, Colorado

It is always noon at Mesa Verde. Even for others, the light is a shock. Like hostages changing safe houses we trudge up and down the cliff staircases of the Anasazi, a clever prehistoric people bent on surviving the light. They came over the cliffs, built the staircases, sank wells for enemies, then left. Light stayed. "I wonder, will our house last this long?" says a hostage from Minneapolis. "We live right in the middle of town." The emperor is videotaping shoes and trousers of other hostages. He is appalled by the crowd conditions but pleased when I point out we are the dirtiest people here. *Who stands near the ink gets black,* says classical Chinese wisdom. Whir. Click. Do you believe me about the light? Whir click. Look at the trees. The bark. Click. It flays it.

Mesa Verde, Colorado

The Anasazi were their own hostages. Clothing was simple, they dressed in hunger and woe. Moving sideways along their bitter balconies. Yucca fibers shred open in the winter wind blasting down that canyon. We know nothing about them but facts. They ate corn, beans, squash, corn, beans, squash, corn, beans, squash, corn, beans, squash and once in a while a wild green onion. They covered the mesa with towers and tunnels in patterns no one can read and periodically set fire to them for a reason no one has guessed, so it is called religious. There are a few glyphs. Glyphs are cuts in rock. Anthropologists interpret them in ways that lock and come apart and lock again. Here is a glyph the anthropologists call Orpheus, it has a lyrelike object in one hand and its heart is cliffs, with dwellings on them, many visible ones and some abandoned. I am stopped a ways off from the emperor to watch him videotape Orpheus. Love comes hungering along the canyon. It will give you pleasure if you believe it.

Mesa Verde, Colorado

Camping soon will end. There I am on shore, a big liner is passing far out at sea and waves are arriving at my feet, soon all will be blank again. I lived blank for many years. And learned two things. Enlightenment is useless and nothing replaces the sting of love, for good or ill. Three things. *A wise badger has three burrows.* Nonetheless you can live fairly easily up there and fill thick notebooks, lying on top of the wall, like Kafka the night his father put him on the *pavlatche*. He viewed the stars and listened to the family inside at dinner. Too much nakedness in them, he decided. He may have meant the stars.

Mesa Verde, Colorado

Badger House is the name of the most imposing complex structure left by the Anasazi at Mesa Verde, with tower tunnel forty-one feet long. When it burned, both entrances were open. Flames drawn through the tunnel some twenty feet toward the tower charred the roof and consumed a man walking along there about A.D. 900, whose skeleton was found by anthropologists in 1958. Why Badger House has this name is unknown. No one has seen a badger hereabouts for centuries and burrowing animals play no part in Anasazi glyphs or legends. The emperor is more interested in the question where we might find a wild green onion to fry up for supper with the leftover chicken. We are tracking illicitly through the piñon trees and duck out of sight when the ranger's truck goes by loaded with hostages.

I was never good at cooking or interested in cultivation. Men who do these things fill me with tenderness. I have watched him in his dahlia garden bending over them with care. Nature has laws and men live by them, men love nothing else that well.

Lachine, Quebec

Dahlias, now. A raw yardful of dahlias—we are making our way through them toward the street. A morning. After the first night I slept at his house, which, as you know and he does not, is the first night I slept at any man's house. Through the wet grass, walking behind him. All of a sudden he stops and bends aside. Snaps off a single dark red dahlia, my eyes going out of me like a cry. Lover, I thought. Now he keeps going and reaches his car and jumps in, placing the dahlia on the seat beside him, drives off. With a wave. My car is parked farther down the street.

Mesa Verde, Colorado

The theory I am happy with is that the Anasazi themselves were badgers.

I wanted to tell a story purely in the style of Samuel Beckett or simple industrial noise, that is the sort of storytelling we like nowadays. Details are in bad taste, they expose our infection. Just before becoming infected we invented anthropology to house our details. This science of man, which is always about other people, whose details are exotic, calms us and opens out the further possibility of anthropologizing ourselves. Hence modern love. Well enlightenment is useless but I find interesting the distinction anthropologists make between an *emic* and an *etic* point of view. Emic has to do with the perspective of a member of the society itself and etic is the point of view of an outsider seeing the society in his own terms. Lovers—correct me if I'm wrong—insist on bringing the two perspectives together, a sort of double exposure. To draw into the very inside of my heart the limit that was supposed to mark it on the outside, your strangeness. But keep it strange. Those three things.

Outside the mind there is no badger sutra, outside the badger sutra there is no mind, wrote the classical P'an master with a brush made out of a badger's tail.

Mesa Verde, Colorado

Life is points on a journey, it seems generally agreed. Between the apriorities howl strong winds. Yet the traveler, once in a long while, comes to a place he is sure, without a doubt in his mind, never having seen it before, is the one he was seeking. He enters. At first everything inside is so saturated with strangeness it is hard to breathe—but look now: already it is drying in from the edges like rainwater in the March wind and he will in fact never after be able to recover that blankness in which he saw it first, the surgery of first look. That moment of pure anthropology.

My first impression of you, a storm-dark night, crowded cocktail party, Billie Holiday on the radio. Sitting straight-backed on a straight-backed chair, the long white hands crossed at the wrist. Good he is homosexual, I thought and began to talk to him about inks. *Was so indescribably new.*

Mesa Verde, Colorado

Camping is a pattern that locks and comes apart and locks again, like Aristotle's principle of noncontradiction. For the same thing both to hold and not to hold of the same thing at the same time and in the same manner is impossible, says Aristotle. Hot in the tent and very early. Outside the sun is up and naked. I can hear the hostage in the next tent begin to undo the zipper of his sleeping bag. It snags. You must think me heartless. A person who did not find sexual intercourse human would be far from being a pleasant being, says Aristotle. *Make me your boy slut.* The emperor's voice is a dark coil, the taste of it heats my brain. Natural language is as brittle as pearl and the principle of noncontradiction too basic to be demonstrated, Aristotle avows, it can only be refuted. A single counterexample will do. Up, Daruma.

Colorado, Route 89

Like two particles in a complex sentence we sit side by side moving forward, eyes on the road. Parataxis is a charged instant of language cold on the surface, unexplained underneath. Let my courage not abandon me. *Body and shadow comfort one another,* says classical Chinese wisdom. I spent much of my childhood staring straight ahead at the hood of a car and America unrolling to the horizon. Father too drove with eyes on the road. Stop the tape and look at these people, one young and one old. Like two stars hung in a deep wind in space, who appear motionless as they hurtle toward each other at 186,213 miles per second in a silence that cracks a wall.

Colorado, Route 90

Blue sky hammers us toward Utah. Falling-rock zone. Loud radio, women in a love shack with men who cannot pretend. Desert begins. Light peels your eyelids back. We bleach along roads plucked dry as the notes of a xylophone.

Colorado, Ute Land

"Here, look at the map and tell me where we are." He hands me the map. My heart sinks. I glance out at the gravel desert into which we are headed, its own waterless ocean. Sky so blue it comes off on your eyes. I see shadows in the process of being sucked back into the light. I see no main road in any direction. "How far are we from the main road?" His voice cuts across the static from the radio. Meanwhile the truck is battering forward from rut to rut over desert-rock gristle, silk pavilions lashed tight, boulders flying up. "Are you in a hurry for some reason?" He does not answer. We hit a pothole, tilt, back up, go crashing on—yet the fact is, the landscape seems to be slowing down around us. Boulders as big as a two-man tent balance gradually on the shadowless ground. Rocks splashed revenge black come to a halt along the roadside one after another. Light stops everywhere in the air. To whom does our action belong, even at the best of times? From the radio comes a voice that sounds like Ray Charles singing Chinese. Perhaps I am just getting mystical, as my father used to say, but I do not feel at ease here. According to the map, this whole area is a Ute reservation. Well it's true a good concubine is not constrained by objective conditions, she knows how to create a savor in any room or situation, her lighthearted patter will make the guests laugh, make the time pass. But I do not like the words ENTRY FORBIDDEN TO UNAUTHORIZED PERSONS which appear on the map underneath UTE. I glance sideways at the emperor, staring straight ahead he drives like someone answering machine-gun fire. Ute. Thrill. Ute. I can feel the front-end axle under me as it were one of my own bones. It is going to break. It breaks.

Ute sky contains sky. Ute potholes contain potholes. Ute desert contains UNAUTHORIZED PERSONS, it slowly arrives around them and locks. In front of the truck a lone oil rig cranks ghostily up and down in the motionless air.

Luz, Utah

Angry? No, never until after. She is reaching toward him, so happy he has come it doesn't matter why—still dark outside —but look already he is tugging on his coat, glancing toward the street where the taxi idles at the curb and her child arms are rubbery with joy as she kneels up on the bed to take hold of him in the cool starry dawn. "Go back to sleep," he says pushing her lightly. How kind he is. How good he smells. That cold overcoat smell will always remind her of the drug of his person, a person known only in dreams, in real life they never embraced.

By the time I wake, anger is scorching through me, I set off through the desert of the hours of the day. It is already late, there is much to be done. The light snaps at my heels like a farm dog. On the radio Ray Charles is singing, *You took the part that was my heart*. Statistics show that women dream of their fathers 40 percent more frequently than men. *Why not, yes oh why not*. Also that during all sleep states a notably higher degree of hemispheric coherence is demonstrated by female brains than by male. *Why not take all of me*. Neurologists remain uncertain what to do with this data, obtained by accident during experiments with insomniacs. *Take my arms I won't use them, why not oh why not yes why not, take all of me.*

Natural Bridges, Utah

Piles of red planets cover Utah. Pillowing upward like heavily padded kimonos with terraces of green silk. It looks elastic from a distance, mounds of red dough pulled and pocked by what hands of air or ancient ocean? The emperor is jumping from rock to rock ahead of me shouting, *"Two hundred and ten million years old!"* His boy's body sways on the wind. Two hundred and ten million years of desire wash through me. Blood-eater. Suppose I let it escape as seed shoots through the eyes of a dreaming god—would it frighten him away? Men know almost nothing about desire, they think it has to do with sexual activity or can be discharged that way. But sex is a substitute, like money or language. Sometimes I just want to stop seeing.

Hite Marina, Utah

Camping is like marriage—locked, that is what the word means. Those three things. The emperor is eating flapjacks and reading the funnies, as they are called in America. I do not read the funnies—I never get the jokes. He is marking the good ones for me with a pencil. Even so I will have to laugh behind my hand, a concubine's dilemma. Meanwhile out the window of the diner I view the landscape, a numb red moon. What hedonist bathed in these dry oceans, 210 million years deep the gouges of his desire—what was it like, the night he wrapped his legs around Utah? One may also view the funnies upside down, they become small strongly lit boxes of life where Popeye is raising merry heck from stem to stern of the Sea Hag's ship. Belowdecks the Sea Hag sits down to morning tea with Mr. Wimpy. *Good day you wonderful woman. I hope you slept well,* says Mr. Wimpy, lifting his fedora. The Sea Hag pulls Mr. Wimpy close. Looking deep into his round nose she says, *Somehow you thrill me strangely, Mr. Wimpy. You kindle a spark within me which I thought to be dead.* With both hands Mr. Wimpy is holding his fedora behind his back at a polite angle. The Sea Hag's arm is locked around his neck. Mr. Wimpy blinks. *I too thrill at your proximity, you gem of the ocean. Do you by chance happen to have a bit of sandwich handy?* The emperor snaps the newspaper shut. It is time to go and view the petroglyphs of Canyon Reef or whatever other comic strips of prehistory we can find inscribed on Utah like windows into 210 million years of how else. *I beg pardon?* says Mr. Wimpy.

Lake Powell, Utah

There is something profoundly uneventful about a man-made lake, like the self-knowledge of a radical skeptic. We arrived some hours after midnight and fell asleep beside the truck.

Now at dawn the unsouled blank stare of Lake Powell. I stare back. Normally when viewing a landscape you can feel what is moving from mountains to shore to sky to waves and back again. Here there is no conversation. Grayness crouches over the water. ENFORCED 24 / 7 / 365 reads a sign whose upper half has been defaced. And lying on its side in the gravel between the sign and our truck is an enormous concrete block. "Be careful not to hit that when you drive out." I am astonished to hear my father's voice coming out of my mouth. Father used to specialize in this kind of black magic. "Now don't drop that," whenever I picked up a glass. He meant well. It was order that obsessed him and when he began to lose his mind he suffered from this. He would spend all day making lists, lists dropped from his clothing everywhere he moved. Late one evening I picked up a book he had been reading. On the top of the page in pencil, TURN OUT THE LIGHT. He was always a forceful writer. The letters had embossed themselves through three pages underneath.

Zion Canyon, Utah

I try to maintain a remote demeanor amid stunning self-accusations. The videotapes will furnish points of fact—broken tent pegs, badly folded maps, mice in the bread, moody penances—what I am on trial for is betrayal of pleasure. I am very tired; interrogation makes me dull and because I had been able to act on my own for many years have lost my sense of right and wrong. There is a right way and a wrong way to do everything, Father used to say. Well for the moment I am right. Chopping an onion for the emperor to put in our evening omelette. Onions are like diamonds the way they shatter, I am lining up each cut on an axis that runs from my elbow to the planet Venus, just now rising over the campground. "What are you doing with these onions?" His voice is standing above me suddenly. It drops like a net. Looking around I see I have chopped seven onions and am starting an eighth. I was young, it was morning, I was given a vessel to carry and I smashed it. But I do not say this. On the videotape at this point you see a tiny Venus reflected in each of his eyes, then black.

Zion Canyon, Utah

Camping, like religion, will make clear to you your one true enemy. Part of the religious process of leaving Utah is a ritual called "the straight shot." That means we wait all day, depart near sundown, drive across Death Valley by night and arrive in Los Angeles when the dawn is breaking. I like this idea. Yet I find myself arguing lengthily against it, as if that is who I am. The emperor gets very quiet and goes off to sleep in the shade. That is who he is, he can sleep anytime. So the hours of the afternoon slowly pile one on top of another. I sit in the truck, practice shifting gears. Time has a gender; I suppose you know this. For example, the first afternoons of a love affair are some of the longest time in a woman's life. If there is a telephone in the room, it is better not to look at it. But even so, you will have a growing sense of the hours of his afternoon running parallel to your own like a videotape on another channel, and feel them slowly rising up, building up, piling up, one by one until it seems at last they are all balanced there at the top of the light well and ready to drop—straight down wide open to the night. Well enlightenment is useless but I do not like the fact that a shot has a target. We are driving to Los Angeles because he wants to live there. When the ritual is over, campers go their separate ways.

Lachine, Quebec

Language is what eases the pain of living with other people, language is what makes the wounds come open again. I have heard that anthropologists prize those moments when a word or bit of language opens like a keyhole into another person, a whole alien world roars past in some unarranged phrase. You remember Proust so appalled when Albertine lets fall "get her pot broken." Or you hear a Berliner say "squat town"—and suddenly see sunset, winter, lovers cooking eggs in a grimy kitchen with the windows steaming up, river runs coldly by, little cats go clicking over the snow. You can fill your district notebook with these jottings, exciting as the unwary use of a kinship term. Through my acquaintance with the emperor, for example, I have added to my notebook the terms *dick* and *cunt* and *score*, whose lexical meanings I knew before but now I see the usage. The research comes alive in unexpected ways. Tonight as we drive down Route 15, the evening news on the radio brings a story from my hometown, where a man with a hunting rifle walked into a schoolroom and shot fourteen girls dead. The notes in his pocket said he is tired of women, their lips bother him and he couldn't score. Well every person has a wall to go to, every person has heart valves to cure in the cold night air. But you know none of us is pure. You know the anger that language shelters, that love obeys. Those three things. Why obey.

Nevada, Route 15

Baby we got a love deluxe, Ray Charles is singing on the radio. Front wheels somewhat awry ever since the emperor drove over a concrete block in our haste to depart Lake Powell two dawns ago, the straight shot wobbles along Highway 15 at 40 mph. We leave behind Utah. Red rocks. Through Arizona. Black paws of old lava gripping the sides of the road. Into Nevada. Rat-stubble light. Desert syntax is hot and transactional: 700 SUPERLOOSE SLOTS. "They call them tight when they aren't paying off," says the emperor with a glance out at the billboard, then resumes his history of China. In 1539 the northern frontiers of the empire were overrun by Mongol hordes seeking relief from constant drought. Having penetrated as far as the Ta'o River, the Mongols defeated the Fan tribes indigenous to that place, reduced its male population and stayed on to inhabit the river basin. And they decided to cut out the tongues of the Fan women lest their language be corrupted. Then because the women were silenced of their speech while the men spoke on, these people came to be called

P'an (*p'ang fan shen*) which means either "I dreamed" or "pulse without blood."

It is easier to tell a story of how people wound one another than of what binds them together. Be careful of this story-teller's tendency to replace precise separate lines with fast daubs of ink. I know how to fool your mind so that your eye accepts what it did not see. A curtain of wash is not a desert. Where ink bleeds into paper is not an act of love, and yet it is. See.

Death Valley, Nevada

Tight hot knobs of sunset come moaning across the million little rocks of the ground. We are driving with the windows up because it is a hundred degrees in Death Valley. I watch the edge of his face in the dark. Its beauty is part of what binds me to him. I don't know how to make this sound virtuous. The soul rises for many reasons. Some of them like a pure and remote view of mountains and streams. Some of them hot as death. Earlier today we discussed the topic of his doctoral dissertation (concubinage and the concept of the traditional wife) briefly. *Admonitions of the Imperial Preceptress to the Concubines of the Court* is the name of a third-century scroll from which he was reading aloud while I drove, late-afternoon light fuming inside my eyelids in black stars. *Favor must not be abused and love must not be exclusive,* the imperial preceptress reminds us. To me this topic is like unpicking a letter bomb. *Exclusive love breeds coyness and extreme passion is fickle.*

There was so little I could say. My soul is a rough and basic one. Heat feelings come from beauty. Also they come from the thought of other concubines. Well enlightenment is useless but perhaps this would be better expressed in an ink painting where slot machine is a visual pun for *Stop the box*. Meanwhile the emperor is saying something in Chinese and we are speeding across gravel hills and salt flats toward the land of his dreams. *The Tao never flourishes but to deteriorate*—classical Chinese wisdom is firm on this. So the imperial preceptress reminds us. So the emperor repeats. So I tell it to you. The desert has one bowl to fill and to empty. On its pure rim are just now coming into view the gold outlines of coy Las Vegas.

Las Vegas, Nevada

On the radio someone is interviewing Ray Charles. *When I do a song I like to make it stink in my own way,* Ray Charles is saying. With eyes closed I can smell the fickle Tao of Las Vegas heating up in layers. We seem to be driving through the center of town, to judge from the frequency of stops. Traffic intersections smell like underfur of dogs. Raw liver as the humans wash past hot, cold, hot. Neon smells like shock treatment and makes that same ice-pick nick on your mind. I remember on the eve of my thirteenth birthday, I overheard my aunts talking to Father about young girls and the dangerous age. "But she isn't going to be one of them," I heard Father say firmly. I was filled with pride, which smells like rubies. *I got seven nights to rock,* Ray Charles is singing, *got seven nights to roll.* His voice smells like wooden rain. Who will I be instead? is a question I never got around to asking Father. *Every night goin show my face with a different chick in a different place.* Well I suppose I can be anyone I like or rather, with eyes closed, nobody at all. *A dream dreamt in a dreaming world is not really a dream,* says classical Chinese wisdom, *but a dream not dreamt is.*

California, Route 15

It is 3:00 a.m. in the desert. Along the roadside lie gigantic sleeping badgers covered in snow. Brave as bamboo the emperor is holding the car together as we charge the rattling night. I sit fast, perfecting my commitment to compassion and watch the snow breathe up and down. Stars burn. The moon rises and tilts her luscious simple head and swims it across the sky. As we start down the freeway she blinks once, crashes into the skyline of LA and disappears as calmly as the master of classical wisdom, asked to brush "The Thousand Character Essay," wrote out twenty-eight characters, then "I forgot the rest," then stopped. The emperor is happier and happier. We approach the land of his dreams. Lotus grows there. His black brush line tears the paper.

Los Angeles, California

The void opens. It is blank hot hungry dawn on Sunset Boulevard as we rattle down the foreplane of the light. The emperor has one hand on the radio dial, switching from talk show to talk show. *Do I know how love begins? Yes I know how love begins,* says a calm female voice. The emperor switches the station. *Before the evolution of the universe there was a long plane sheet of galaxies, stretching for at least a billion light-years, that scientists call "the great wall." From somewhere distant in space but surprisingly close to the beginning of time, light from a quasar or quasi-stellar object began to arrive. There was a concentration of matter so massive that it was exerting a steady gravitational pull on all the galaxies of the great wall. Scientists call this pull "the great attractor." Some believe in the presence also of exotic particles known as "dark matter" and there were shock waves from exploding stars. A faint ringing sound. The wall got bumpy—*static interrupts the voice, the emperor switches the station. *Do I know how it ends?* He snaps the radio off.

Los Angeles, California

Pain has no meaning. No pure cliffs. Pain is an oven. Where drugs run out and luxury drops away. But for the moment he sleeps. Glistens. The night burns slowly on. Ever on the prowl my desire, which I hate, sits beside the bed. Full moon, the last I will view with him. Already it seems like years and years. Each little thing the entire truth.

Los Angeles, California

During the day I walk the streets of the oven. I should have left days ago. Why do women think they can make things better? When I sit beside him I can feel the pain come through me like print. *The wood is already made into a boat,* says classical Chinese wisdom. Could you have found the cures he needs? On a mat in a shaded squat house he lies with his eyes open. Glistens. Pain is bad for conversation. But men are always in pain, aren't they? in some sense. The mischief of desire is viral in them. How women avoid this suffering is a question I have, without conclusion but not without interest, long entertained. You may say they do not avoid it, yet male concubines are as rare in archetype as in history. At any rate the emperor will have other lovers when I go, it is not a question of loyalty, but of pleasure, he says. I sit on my calm heels and listen to this reasoning, although air seems to have all of a sudden entirely left the region of my lungs and heart. Pleasure is important. Pleasure is a way of knowing people. Pleasure is the infinite experiment. Well before I fell in love I used to reason too. I was a young Fan bandit. I was a bad bone. Stop the box.

Los Angeles, California

Out on the street again, walking fast to nowhere in particular. Noon soaking whitely from under sullen sky pads. In the videotape you can see the woman moving along a crack that runs from front to back of the daylight. Acutance is good. She is reasoning calmly. *Most happiness stops fairly soon,* says classical Chinese wisdom. Deep within the inmost Sylvian fissure of the human cerebrum, visible only when the lips of the fissure are widely separated since it is overlapped and hidden by convolutions of tissue that are its workings, lies the central lobe of the brain, which neurologists call *insula.* That means "island." The woman is gripping hard on this fact. Something so strange and simple. The radical for *within* in classical Chinese is an empty box. You can indicate withinness of any kind you like by setting another radical within the box. For example human love, while it is happening, will seem like something within withinness. (You can indicate this by multiplying the insets to create what Berliners call *das Rot des Roten.*) On the other hand, withinness may spit you out like a glass eye. In that case, you can paint the box black with ink ground yesterday or the day before and call it *Just for the Thrill.*

Los Angeles, California

I've no story to tell. Front face, back of the head, profile. Mug shots. A suspect may recur, he may not. There is a lot to know about love, suppose I withhold as much from you as the emperor of China withheld from me, even in our last hours, will you be content with that bare windowless room? Can you be an optimist about nothing? Try. My power is of the kind that belongs exclusively to those without power. *Not explain-*

able then do not explain it, says classical Chinese wisdom, *not explaining then resolve it without explanation.* An anthropologist's priority is to expose the outside on the inside. It is a tribe lost by finding it, like desire. Like some stained wall where all of a sudden you see a face.

Los Angeles, California

A dark room moves slowly through the hours toward dawn. Last night in camp. The emperor turns, struggles in tides, goes under, sleeps on. Sweat. A cry. Old bits of his blood on the bed, other stains. *Conditions have the same character of water,* says classical Chinese wisdom. Some academicians understand this as a reference to change and changefulness, or meaning that we drown, or tears. Well enlightenment is useless but I think it means that freedom is a way of being burned alive. I saw my father burning, crouched in his cage of blankets, a thousand years old in the black neon noon of the hospital corridor. He was concentrating hard with his mouth and his eyes. He turned to me, fixed me. "Then what?" he said, and he answered himself in a long, traveling whisper. "Fires are the furthest in you are and the worst you are."

Lachine, Quebec

Well you cannot perceive the truth unless you are attending to it. Even so perhaps not. But look here comes the natural light striking in like a dawn, into this room where we lived for a year before our trek, empty now. *Quiet as paper,* says classical

Chinese wisdom. His map of China is still tacked up on the wall. "No you keep that," he said when we were packing.

Appendix on Lady Cheng

Our budget of knowledge about Lady Cheng is scant. She endured violent times and a disturbing century, making no mention of these in private writings. We see her life like a drop running down a wall. It is recorded that her father was of the Fan tribes, mother unknown. Nineteen years of service at the imperial court ended for Lady Cheng in exile in 1574. The cause is unknown. She is thought to have returned to China at the time of the emperor's death in 1601, then vanished. An unusually uneven education failed to equip Lady Cheng for the intensely literary life of the Hades court. Her own writings, judged unimpressive, have for the most part not been preserved. But her mapmaking was regarded with interest by both lay persons and scholars, especially the scrolls on which she recorded a delightful trip to the Ta'o River region in 1553. The maps themselves are no longer extant; academicians were quick to point out their uselessness as a source of topographical information for the area. Remarkably ignorant of Chinese geography, Lady Cheng made important mistakes about the places she visited. In fact, to judge from what remains of the list of maps and inscriptions composed to accompany them, Lady Cheng's concern for objective conditions was fitful. Can you read a map by the light of a thunderstorm? *Who stands near the ink gets burned,* says classical Chinese wisdom.

Maps (Ta'o Trek) 1553

1. Capital and Area Around the Capital
2. Cross-Fire Zone
3. Jade Hills
4. Marches
5. Cheng Farm
6. Moon-Viewing Station (Usual)
7. Trout Ponds
8. Buried Trail to Ponds
9. Autonomous Prefecture (Ta'o)
10. Free Zone
11. Flood Storage Area
12. District Line (80th)
13. Unidentified Regional Boundaries
14. Present Frontier
15. Chosen Desert
16. Former Silk Route
17. Temple of the Heavenly Mirror
18. Water-Control Project
19. Flint Hills
20. Devil's Bridge
21. Glacier Fields and Zone of Permanent Ice
22. Ten-Heart Hermitage
23. Coast Road
24. Lookout
25. Tunnels (Entrances)
26. Spring Hermitage
27. Mountain of the Demon Queller

28. Where We Saw the Birds
29. Hills of Heaven
30. Hives
31. Old Frontier
32. Flesh and Blood Bridge
33. Xing Reservoir
34. Burned-Over Land
35. Temple of the Pleasure Barrier
36. Formerly Cultivated Land (Cucumber)
37. Fort
38. Cells (Unknown Sect)
39. Wells
40. Tableland
41. Third Elevation
42. New Cultivated Land (Onion)
43. Hothouses (Imperial)
44. Foreign Canton Within Ta'o Prefecture
45. Foreshore
46. Hot Springs
47. Poles of Our Defense
48. Teahouse (Access)
49. Teahouse (Ground Plan)
50. Toll Gates with Locks
51. Tide Gauges
52. Salt Meadows and Kilns
53. Stolen Lake (Access Omitted)
54. Judges Gate
55. Slow Pools
56. Old Capital

57. Straight Road
58. Bridge of Just Tears
59. Stations of Refreshment for Travelers on the Straight Road
60. Hill of Lucky Observance
61. Entire Ta'o Basin (To Scale)
62. Moon-Viewing Station (Unusual)
63. Custom House
64. The Island
65. Shrine of the Strange Pairing
66. Place Where We Lost Two Tents (Fire)
67. Great Wall

Inscriptions

> *Of the inscriptions, one survives intact, along with some fragments cited by a later academician on a point of dialect. Translations are literal.*

Heaven and hell are illusions of one another unbending stiff knees at dawn can we laugh at demons together we two?

(Map 31)

On her back over the lake

Click

The Wishing Jewel:
Introduction to Water Margins

> *Brother (noun) associate, blood brother, cadet, colleague,*
> *fellow,* frater, frère, *friar, kinsman, sibling, soul brother,*
> *twin brother. See CLERGY, FRIEND, KINSHIP.*
>
> Roget

My brother once showed me a piece of quartz that contained, he said, some trapped water older than all the seas in our world. He held it up to my ear. "Listen," he said, "life and no escape."

This was a favorite phrase of his at that time. He had dropped out of high school to do martial arts and his master liked to say "life and no escape" when translating the Chinese word *qi,* which means "breath" or "energy" and is fundamental to good kicks. I remember we were down by the lake, it was sunset, fireboat clouds were lining up on the horizon. He was doing his Mountain Movements / Sea Movements exercises. "Pervasive but you can't see it, physical but has no body." His left foot flashed past my head. "*Qi* is like water, the master says, we float on the water when the level is right everything swims." His right foot cut the air to ribbons. "Put it in your mind you've got a wishing jewel." It was cold sitting there in the November wind but I liked being with him. We had survived a lot together. It's true he hated me all through childhood—for my ugliness, he had explained simply, and this seemed reasonable enough. But around the age of fourteen hatred gave way to unexpected days of truce, perhaps because I caught up to him in school and was affable about doing his homework. Who cares why. A sun came out on my life. We spent a lot of time that winter driving around town in his truck listening to the radio and talking about Dad or sex. Well, he talked.

His stories were all about bad luck. It wasn't his fault that headlights got smashed, the school flunked him, his girlfriend thought she was pregnant, the police arrested him for driving naked on the beach. But good luck, he felt, was just around the corner. He was someone bound for happiness and he knew where to find it. He knew he was close. Very close. As I listened to him a sadness began in me that I have never quite put down. Still, it pleased me that he thought I was smart and asked my opinions about things. He called me Professor and gave me Roget's *Thesaurus* in the deluxe two-volume edition for Christmas. It is here beside me, volume one at least. He never got around to giving me volume two.

For some reason, he believed in me. "She's going to be someone you know," he said to my mother once. I heard this from her only after he was gone. It was late spring when he disappeared, for reasons having partly to do with the police, partly with my father—it doesn't matter now. Postcards came to us from farther and farther away, Vermont, Belgium, Crete, with long spaces of time in between them. No return address. Then very early one morning, about three years after he left, he called from Copenhagen (collect). I stood on the cold linoleum, listening to a voice that sounded like him in a padded costume. Layers and layers of hard times and resentment crusted on it. He had got his front teeth knocked out in a fight and needed a large sum for dentistry. He asked me to send money and not to tell Dad. After he hung up it took several moments to unclench my fingers from the telephone.

A card came from Copenhagen after I wired the money. He was on his way east, heading for China. Cards came from Paris and then from Marseilles—I remember that one, it was his birthday and he was buying drinks for everyone in the bar. A card came from Israel, rather sadder. A card came from Goa, mentioning heat and dirt and the monsoon delayed. Then no more cards came.

I don't reckon my brother ever got to China. So I made him a wishing jewel.

Water Margins:
An Essay on Swimming by My Brother

Friday 4:00 a.m. Not swimming.

Black motionless night. Bushes. The swimmer stands at the window. Ducks are awake down by the water's edge.

Friday 4:00 p.m. Swimming.

In late afternoon the lake is shaded. There is the sudden luxury of the places where the cold springs come flooding up around the swimmer's body from below like an opening dark green geranium of ice. Marble hands drift enormously in front of his face. He watches them move past him down into the lower water where red stalks float in dust. A sudden thin shaft of fish smell. No sleep here, the swimmer thinks as he shoots along through the utterly silent razor-glass dimness. One drop of water entirely awake.

Saturday 6:30 a.m. Swimming.

At dawn a small mist cool as pearls hangs above the lake. The water is dark and waits in its motionless kingdoms. Bars of light proceed diagonally in front of the swimmer as he moves forward following the motions of the strange white hands. Gold rungs slide past beneath. Red water plants waver up from the bottom in an attitude of plumes. How slow is the slow trance of wisdom, which the swimmer swims into.

Saturday 9:00 a.m. Swimming.

The swimmer prowls among the water lilies at the water's edge. Each has a different smell (orange, honey, milk, rot, clove, coin) like people. He is putting his nose into one calyx after another, wondering if they compete for him when an insect of the type called a darning needle rows into his eyelashes. Rival suitor. The swimmer backpaddles and moves hugely on his way, through underwater courts of brides swaying the wonderful red feathers of their legs as lengths of visible secret. The water mounts pleasures at him through every doorway. Exposed. He swims off.

Sunday 8:00 a.m. Swimming.

A Sunday flood of hot lights pound down onto the black glass of the lake. The swimmer is grateful to escape underneath to where his dim water kingdom receives him. Silently. Its single huge gold nod. Who else ever knew me? the swimmer thinks. The hand with the wedding ring floats down past his face and disappears. No one.

Thursday 12:00 p.m. Swimming.

At noon the water is a cool bowl where the swimmer drops and darts away from the broiling air. He aligns himself and moves forward with his face in the water staring down at the bottom of the lake. Old, beautiful shadows are wavering steadily across it. He angles his body and looks up at the sky. Old, beautiful clouds are wavering steadily across it. The swimmer thinks about symmetries, then rotates himself to swim on his back staring at the sky. Could we be exactly wrong about such things as—he rotates again—which way is up? High above him he can feel the clouds watching his back, waiting for him to fall toward them.

Thursday 5:00 p.m. Swimming.

The swimmer lets himself fall out of the day heat and down through a gold bath of light deepening and cooling into thousands of evenings, thousands of Augusts, thousands of human sleeps. He is thinking of the light that sinks about her face in Leonardo's painting called *The Virgin of the Rocks.* Once he saw her kneeling by the water. Now he plunges along through the cold rock colors of the lake. Halos are coursing over the ridged mud of the bottom. He dives to get one. *If ever I forget my deep bond to you.*

Monday 5:30 a.m. Swimming.

Blue peaches are floating down onto the lake from under dawn cloud. The swimmer parts the water like a dancer peeling a leotard down her long opal leg. Sullen where he moves through its unlit depths—a smell of gasoline makes him stop and look around. A small silent rowboat is passing, two women in fishing hats studying him. Old ballerinas, he decides abruptly and dives out of sight.

Monday 12:00 p.m. Swimming.

Noon darkness clamps down on the lake. The water feels black enough to dye his skin. Its cold pressure. A strange greening on top of the water. The swimmer is trying to remember a sentence from Rilke about the world one beat before a thunderstorm—

Monday 6:00 p.m. Swimming.

Rain continues. The far hills are gun-colored with ancient mist floating whitely before them. Chilly and concentrating hard the swimmer moves along just under the surface of the water, watching each drop hit the surface and bounce. Ping. Water on water. He is wondering how it would feel to be a voice in a medieval motet, not a person singing but a voice itself, all the liquors raining and unraining around it. Ping. Or to be a cold willow girl in the ancient hermit's embrace. High above him at the top of the sky, blood clouds are gathering like a wound behind flesh.

Monday 10:00 p.m. Not swimming.

Standing at the window the swimmer stares out through a stretching pitch-black wind toward the lake. He can feel it lift and turn like a sleeper in the same bed. Can hear the wind touch each link of its dreams in between. What does a lake dream? Ping.

Friday 4:00 a.m. Not swimming.

Staring. The lake lies like a silver tongue in a black mouth.

Friday 8:00 a.m. Swimming.

The storm has cleared. A blinding gold wind knocks hard waves flat across the swimmer's face as he plunges forward, trying to place himself in the trough of it but the diagonals shift and mock him. On the surface the water is navy blue and corrugated by wind. Spots of white foam crowd hectically up and down the waves. There is an urgency to it as if a telephone were ringing in the house. But there is no telephone in the house.

Friday 6:00 p.m. Swimming.

A dark blue wind is driving sunset home. The swimmer glances from under his arm at the shoreline where poplar trees are roaring with light and dropping their leaves to silver in the wind. With each stroke of his arm the swimmer exchanges this din for the silence beneath, his sliding green kingdom of hungers, monotonies and empty penetrations. To open this treasury is not for one's father or brother or wife to decide. Oneself.

Wednesday 8:30 a.m. Swimming.

Small white bundles of mist are hurrying over the still surface of the lake. I wonder why I don't dream anymore, the swimmer is thinking as he inserts himself into the dark green glass. There were times he used to dream a lot. Now the nights are blank, except for intervals when he rises to look at the lake. And then behind his back he can feel the cat wake and observe him from its lit eyes. Not lifting its head. It is a very old cat (a gift from his brother) and seems to be dying. Before they go back to sleep he gives the cat a drink from a teacup of water in which he has dissolved some drops of honey. It eats little solid food nowadays but dreams well at night, so far as he can judge from its mutters and tiny thrashings. What unaccountable longings and hidden fears are swimming on fire in you? he wonders as he leans on the bed in the dark watching the small fur body. Almost everything physiologists know about the living brain has been learned from sleeping cats. Sleeping or waking, cat brains most resemble human brains in design. Cat neurons fire as intensely as human neurons, whether bombarded from without or from within. Lightly, lightly he touches its head where the suffering bones come haunting through old flesh. A glow enters his fingers, as if it were a pearl dreaming.

Wednesday 5:45 p.m. Swimming.

The lake is cool and rippled by an inattentive wind. The swimmer moves heavily through an oblique greenish gloom of underwater sunset, thinking about his dull life. Wondering why it doesn't bother him. It bothered everyone else including his father who died, his brother who left the country and his wife who married again. "Why don't you do something?" they would say. "Call someone? What about Pons? What about Yevgeny? Don't you paint anymore?" The swimmer would glance out at the lake lying like a blue thigh in the open gold breeches of the noon sun and forget to answer. Only the cat does not question his lack of events. Where there is nothing to watch, it watches nothing. Perhaps I am the cat's dream, the swimmer thinks, breaking the surface.

Monday 5:00 a.m. Not swimming.

Watching from the window. When they are brand-new ballet shoes have this same sheen of pink and silver, as a lake glinting deep in the fringe of its leaves just before dawn. The cat stirs and groans. Behind its tight shut eyes millions of neurons are firing across the visual cortex. The swimmer bends down. A low rustle of longing sinks from the cat's small open mouth. Neurophysiologists think dreams begin in the brain stem, a box of night perched above the spinal column that also regulates such primitive functions as body temperature and appetite. The swimmer imagines himself dropping into the silent black water of that primitive lake. Shocks of fire flash and die above his head. The cold paints him. All at once he realizes it is not up to him, whether he drowns. Or why.

Friday 4:00 a.m. Not swimming.

The lake is a narrow fume of white mist still as a sleeping face in its dark bowl of leaves. One star hangs above. There is silver from it falling directly into the swimmer's eye. He glances at the cat asleep on the bed like a pile of dropped twigs. Looks back at the lake.

Friday 4:20 a.m. Swimming.

As he approaches the water's edge through soaked grasses he sees the mist open. He stops. Poised before him in the bluing air is a kingfisher heron almost as tall as himself. It is staring out over the lake. As the swimmer watches without breathing, the kingfisher totters profoundly forward from one red leg to another, then all of a sudden gathers itself and in a single pensive motion vanishes through a hole in the mist. The hole closes. The swimmer stands a moment, then drops, down through the dark blue mirror of the lake, to search for red legs and balancings and memories of the way people use love.

Saturday 8:00 a.m. Not swimming.

Robbed sentenced speechless. Bombarded like Sokrates by voices of law from within, the swimmer awakens suddenly feeling like the wrong side of a wing flipped up in the wind. The morning sun is hitting him straight in the eye. From where he lies he can see the lake like a flat plane of gold. A hardworking blue Saturday wind pushing white cloud rags into their places on the sky. The cat is gone.

Saturday 1:00 p.m. Not swimming.

A white eyelid of cloud has closed over the lake. The swimmer stands at the water's edge watching the surfaces of the water blacken and begin to move. Little starts of wind arrive from this direction and from that. Something is being loaded into the air from behind. The swimmer wonders about being struck by lightning. Who will feed the cat? Will his wife come to the funeral? Get hold of yourself, he thinks, but even in childhood he found Saturdays depressing, too porous, not like other days. He wonders where the cat has got to.

Saturday 3:00 p.m. Not swimming.

No storm yet. The air has the pressure and color of fresh-cut granite. Black lake surface is moving, keeps moving, slightly, all over. As if some deep underwater clocks were being wound slowly into position for a moment of revelry. *That she and I may grow old together.* The swimmer turns and goes back up toward the house.

Saturday 5:00 p.m. Not swimming.

No storm. The water stares.

Thursday 7:30 a.m. Swimming.

White motionless mist and the steady screens of rain. A medieval city indicates itself ghostily on the opposite shore. The swimmer stands at the water's edge, listens, feels his ears fill with whiteness and time slip back a notch. He enters the water and begins to swim, placing himself between the black breasts of the water so that his stroke rolls him from wave to wave. The shore moves past. A mountain comes into view. In glimpses from under his arm the swimmer studies this unknown mountain. He sees huge blue pine trees and soaked rocks and white innards of mist hanging and trailing. From between roots a bit of fire. Beside this fire some strange and utterly simple soul keeping watch with its neck drawn into its shoulders. Nipples darken the paper robe. Roasting horse chestnuts and feeding them to something hunched on the log by its side. When the swimmer gets back to the house he finds the cat collapsed on the foot of the bed. Its wet fur smells vile.

Monday 4:30 p.m. Swimming.

A disconsolacy seeps out of the gray light and wanders on the gray water. Cold ripples in series move toward shore. Somewhere up the hill, a chain saw chews into the air then stops. Silence comes lapping back. Shivering like a child the swimmer wades into the water. Childhood is nice in some ways, he thinks. Someone to hold a big towel and wrap you when you come out is nice. As he strikes off along the shore, gray waves slapping at his face, the swimmer thinks about his father holding out the big towel and bundling it around him and murmuring, "Do your best, do your best" in his slightly wild way. The lake wind whipping at them.

Friday 8:45 a.m. Swimming.

The lake is a cold lead pane. Clouds and trees look saddened or dark. But underneath the water an odd verdigris glow is soaking out from somewhere. The swimmer swims along through rooms mysteriously lit as an early Annunciation. Stillness rushes everywhere. It is awake. It knows him and it cares nothing—yet to be known is not nothing. Sometimes the cat will look up suddenly with its eyes like two holes that pin him. *The world where we live is a burning house,* the eyes say. The swimmer glides deeper, thinking about the difference between fullness and emptiness. A few times it happened when he sat in the audience watching her dance that his wife's eyes came to rest on him—empty. He saw right to the back of her head. Modigliani would paint out the iris, which seemed to him too intimate.

Friday 10:00 p.m. Not swimming.

Over the unmoving black body of the lake the moon dreams its gold dream of life, as if it were alone in the world and what dreamer is not?

Sunday 10:30 p.m. Not Swimming.

Freud learned about dreams from watching freshwater crabs which, he saw, were trying to disguise their twitches. The swimmer touches the cat ever so lightly on the bald spot in front of its ear. "For some must watch," he whispers. The cat is looking out from very far back in its eyes now, from a huge room where everything is running slowly away. On the other hand death, yes stealthy enough, ignores no one and never sleeps. The swimmer's tears run down his hand onto the bald spot quiet now. "And some must sleep." The soul of a cat is mortal. It does its best.

Some of the material in this work was originally published in the following:

"Mimnermos: The Brainsex Paintings (Translation, Essay, Interview)" in *Raritan Review*

"Canicula di Anna" in *Quarterly Review of Literature Poetry Series VI*

Selections from "The Fall of Rome: A Traveller's Guide" in *Canadian Literature, North Dakota Quarterly,* and *Pequod*

"Kinds of Water" in *Grand Street* and subsequently in *The Best American Poetry of 1990*

Selections from "Short Talks" in *Bomb, Planetarium Station, The Southwest Review, The Yale Review,* and subsequently in *Brick Books* and *The Best American Poetry of 1992*

"Swimming: An Essay" in *Descant*

"Water Margins" in *The Journey Prize Anthology*